VICTORIAN
FOOTBALL
MISCELLANY

The

VICTORIAN
FOOTBALL
MISCELLANY

By PAUL BROWN

Goal-Post

Published in 2013 by Goal-Post
An imprint of Superelastic

www.superelastic.co.uk

ISBN-13: 9780956227058

Cover image from Sketches at the International Football
Match by William Ralston, the Graphic, 1872.

For more information and content go to:

www.victorianfootball.co.uk

AUTHOR'S NOTES AND ACKNOWLEDGMENTS

Although by definition miscellaneous, it is intended that the various items in this Miscellany will add up to provide an overall history of Victorian football. In an effort to provide some logical structure, the items in the book have generally been arranged in chronological order. For the purpose of the book, 'Victorian era' refers to the period from Queen Victoria's ascension in June 1837 until her death in January 1901.

Sources for this book included hundreds of contemporary newspaper and periodical articles. Efforts have been made to name sources as they are used. Useful books and websites are referenced in the Further Reading section. Thanks to library and archive staff for their assistance, and also to Jonathan Hayden.

Special thanks to Louise for tolerating my football obsession, particularly when my team loses.

www.stuffbypaulbrown.com
www.twitter.com/paulbrownUK

ALSO AVAILABLE

Goal-Post: Victorian Football
Edited by Paul Brown, available as paperback and eBook

A new anthology collecting the very best Victorian football writing, covering the birth and development of the world's greatest game, written by those who were there to witness it. This is a collection of contemporary articles and extracts featuring some of the players, officials, clubs and matches that helped shape and define football. Vol. 2 coming soon.

www.victorianfootball.co.uk

c.350 BC: The Ancient Greeks play a game called *episkyros*, a violent form of football that allows handling. Documented in writings and artwork, it is also referred to as 'battle ball'.

c.250 BC: A kicking game, known as *tsu' chu* or *cuju* (kickball), is played in Han Dynasty China. It involves kicking a fur-stuffed ball through a small hole in a silk cloth.

c.100 BC: The Ancient Romans play several ball games, including *follis*, or balloon-ball, and *harpastum*, a kicking game derived from the Greek *episkyros*. Some historians believe the Romans brought *harpastum* to Britain c.50 AD.

828 AD: The important Anglo-Saxon text *Historia Brittonum* includes the first reference to football in Britain, mentioning 'a party of boys playing at ball'.

c.1180: Canterbury monk William FitzStephen writes that boys 'annually upon Shrove Tuesday go into the fields and play the well-known game of ball'.

1314: The Mayor of London bans 'hustling over large foot balls' in public areas of the city 'on pain of imprisonment'.

c. 1389: Richard II outlaws 'all playing at tennis, football and other games' in the belief that they encourage idleness.

1409: Henry IV bans the levying of money on 'foetball'.

c. 1500: Italians play a complicated kicking game called *calcio*.

1526: Henry VIII orders a pair of football boots.

c.1595 and 1605: William Shakespeare references football in both *A Comedy of Errors* and *King Lear*. (From *Lear*: Steward: 'I'll not be strucken, my lord.' Kent: 'Nor tripped neither, you base football player.')

1755: Dr Samuel Johnson's *Dictionary of the English Language* contains the entry: 'FOOTBALL: A ball commonly made of a blown bladder. The sport or practice of kicking a football.'

1801: Historian Joseph Strutt writes a description of the game, beginning with: 'Football is so called because the ball is driven about with the feet instead of the hands.'

c. 1815: Poet Walter Scott writes two songs about a football match in Scotland: '...And life itself is but a game at football.'

THE MOB GAME

Football was a common pastime at the beginning of the Victorian era. Indeed, reports of the festivities surrounding the coronation of Queen Victoria in 1837 mention several celebratory football matches. The game, however, was very different to the football we know today. The most prevalent 'organised' form of football was the folk or 'mob' game, played in towns and villages across the country. Matches would often be played on holidays and other special occasions. Several towns arranged games on Shrove Tuesday, which was traditionally a half-day holiday. As a result, the mob game is sometimes referred to as Shrovetide football. Games could involve hundreds of players, with a village's men-folk divided into two teams according to various attributes such as height, age or marital status. Inter-village matches were also common, adding a dash of local rivalry to the mix. Rules differed by region, but typically goals (or gates) would be set up a fair distance apart, often at each end of the village. The ball would be 'thrown up' to start the match, and each team would attempt to 'drive' it through their opponents' goal. The first team to score a goal would win the game. This could last all day, and would often take its toll on the players (and the village). It was a hectic and violent game, with tripping and kicking at shins allowed, and there were many broken legs and other injuries. Fatalities weren't uncommon, and there are numerous reports of matches turning into riots. There is an account of a French visitor who, on observing a village game, remarked that if the English called this playing, it would be impossible to say what they would call fighting. He was referring to a Shrovetide match that is still played annually at Ashbourne, Derbyshire, between the 'up'ards' and 'down'ards'. The village football tradition also endures in Alnwick, Northumberland. This Shrovetide match was originally played between the married men and the single men of the town, with a cash prize provided for the winners by the Duke of Northumberland.

PUNISHABLE OFFENCE

Before football was codified, and before pitches were marked out, the game was played in the streets. As a result, it was not uncommon to see masses of men and boys charging through towns and villages up and down the country, causing much bedlam and disorder, in pursuit of a football. Normal life was disrupted, windows were broken, and citizens were trampled. There were regular arrests and trials involving football-related disturbances and breaches of the peace, ranging from noise and obstruction to destruction of private property, with plenty of violence thrown in, too. The Highway Act of 1835 had actually outlawed the playing of football on public highways, 'with a maximum penalty of 40 shillings'. (Playing football on a highway 'to the annoyance of a user' is still prohibited today.) In 1848, the *Sportsman's Gazette* published this advice: 'The game of football is not illegal if played in a fit and proper place, but of course if it is practised in public thoroughfares, creating a disturbance and obstruction, it then becomes a punishable offence.' This crackdown on street games was instrumental in football becoming a field game.

EARLY RISERS

One of the first recorded clubs formed with the intention of playing football was the Early Risers, which is known to have existed in Newcastle upon Tyne in 1848. The club's remit actually went beyond football – and beyond sport. The Early Risers met on the town moor at six o'clock every morning, and would play football, cricket and quoits, and also listen to lectures from guest speakers. Afterwards, members would 'repair to breakfast with an appetite of 40 ploughman-power'. Other early Victorian clubs that are known to have played football in the 1840s included the Great Leicestershire Cricket and Football Club, Surrey Football Club, and Rochdale's the Body-Guard Club.

ANIMAL BLADDERS

The first Victorian footballs were inflated animal bladders, usually ox bladders, although pig bladders were often easier to get hold of via local butchers. The bladders were enclosed in leather cases, typically stitched together by shoemakers, and laced with leather thongs. The finished 'casers' were hard and heavy, and early examples were more oval-shaped than round. India rubber bladders began to be used in the 1860s, although they were initially considered inferior to those made from animal organs. 'They are very pretty to look at, but are sadly liable to burst, while the least wound from a thorn or splinter ruins them at once, for they cannot be mended except by the makers,' wrote George Forrest in 1862. As football increased in popularity, leatherworkers, saddle-makers and tanners began to diversify into football manufacture. Soon, footballs were being made on a large scale, with factories producing balls from rubber and hides. The first officially-approved football was sold by sporting goods retailer Fred Lillywhite. The Lillywhites No 5 ball was selected by the Football Association and the Sheffield Football Association for a match between the two in 1866. The same ball was used for the first FA Cup tournament in 1871, and size 5 (27-28 inches in circumference) has been the regulation size for adult footballs ever since. The Lillywhites sporting goods chain was founded in 1863 and still exists today – now owned by Mike Ashley's Sports Direct.

BLOWING OUT

In March 1840, police were called to deal with a rowdy game of football in Richmond town centre. Five men were arrested, 'for an assault on the police, by obstructing them in the execution of their duty, in kicking the ball'. Also, according to *The Charter* newspaper, 'a lad, Alfred Bayley, aged 16, was apprehended in the act of blowing out a bullock's bladder'.

The Football Game, 1839

FOOTBALL ART

Thomas Webster's *The Football Game*, painted in 1839, was one of the very first works of art to celebrate the game. The oil-on-canvas painting, depicting a gang of boys clambering over each other in rowdy pursuit of the ball (with a tiny 'goalkeeper' in imminent danger of being flattened), was highly praised at the time, and reproductions sold like hot plum puddings. 'An excellent display of juvenile hilarity, humour and character,' the *Morning Chronicle* surmised. 'In composition, colour and expression it is admirable.' Webster (1800-86) was one of the most famous fine artists of the Victorian era. He sold the painting at a Royal Academy exhibition to a Mr Vernon for 200 guineas, equivalent to around £18,000 today. It's now on display at the National Football Museum.

FOOTBALL MURDER

In 1840, James Wilkinson was sent to the House of Correction for two months for the crime of playing football in the streets of Colne, Lancashire. The town's annual Shrovetide match had a reputation for descending into violence, and the local authorities were determined to put an end to it. In 1841, the game turned into a riot, and Wilkinson was again at the centre of it. Around 70 special constables, armed only with truncheons, were attacked by a mob of 200 men armed with metal bars and stones. One constable, Joseph Halstead, was beaten to death with an iron pole. 'In a very few moments his brain was actually battered out,' the *Blackburn Standard* reported. Wilkinson was identified by witnesses and arrested for murder. On the way to prison he told police that he had done it because the constable was the same man who had arrested him 12 months earlier for playing football. However, Wilkinson was eventually acquitted of the constable's murder. His associate Richard Boothman was found to have struck the killer blow, and received the death penalty. Wilkinson was sentenced to 18 months in prison with hard labour.

ON THIN ICE

Ice-skating on frozen ponds and rivers was a popular Victorian pastime, and so, according to multiple newspaper accounts, was playing football on ice. In 1840, the *Morning Chronicle* reported that a large group of men and boys had been playing football on London's Serpentine when the ice had broken under their feet. 'Upwards of a dozen men and boys were struggling for their lives,' the paper reported, explaining how they were rescued with boats, ropes and ladders, and taken away for warm baths and other remedies. 'All were restored to life, with one exception, a lad who had been at least six minutes under the water.' David Caird, aged just 14, 'was removed in a shell to the dead-house'.

SOCCER SOMNAMBULISM

In November 1838, the *Northern Star* reported a curious case of football-related 'somnambulism', or sleepwalking, at a house in Oldham Road in Leeds. 'One night this week, a young lad got up in his sleep, and after going many times round the room, fell down the stairs and knocked out his neck, which so affrighted his mother that it caused premature labour,' the newspaper reported. 'By assistance being at hand the neck was pulled in again, and when recovering his senses, he stated he thought he was playing at football, and in running after it, fell down the stairs.'

ST PATRICK'S DAY RIOT

A St Patrick's Day football match ended in a violent riot in Edinburgh in March 1840. The match, in Holyrood Park, was an annual event played between Irish residents of the town. 'They have been in the habit of assembling for that purpose for several years past, but on this occasion a quarrel broke out amongst them, which ended in a general fight,' reported the *Edinburgh Observer*. 'Sticks and stones were pretty freely used, and, the matter becoming serious, the two or three policemen in attendance thought it time to interfere. No sooner did they advance for this purpose then the mob, abandoning their former quarrel, fell together upon the policemen, attacked them in the most brutal manner, and, having knocked them down, kicked them on various parts of the body.' The policemen were seriously injured, and one, an Officer Ford, was left fighting for his life. 'A reinforcement of the police soon dispersed the cowardly assailants,' reported the newspaper. 'Four of the ringleaders, we are happy to say, are in custody.'

FOOTBALL BANNED

Football was banned in Derby in 1846. The Derby game, traditionally played across Shrove Tuesday and Ash Wednesday for more than a hundred years, was renowned as one of the most violent in the land. 'Playing – as it is not very rationally called – at football in the public streets and thoroughfares is a great public nuisance,' commented the *Derby Mercury*. The town council issued a resolution stating that they would use every means in their power to 'put down football playing'. They printed posters and handbills warning residents not to participate, and swore-in special constables to keep the peace. However, many of the townsfolk remained determined to play, and it became apparent that big trouble was brewing. The council sought advice from the Secretary of State, who called in the military. Nevertheless, the game still went ahead, with its instigator named as Henry Allen. The *Mercury* reported: 'In spite of all these endeavours, and of all these precautionary measures and remonstrations, Allen had thrown up the ball and caused a great and tumultuous assembly, when much riot and confusion ensued, which the civil power was insufficient to suppress.' The Mayor literally read the Riot Act (allowing for anyone who failed to disperse within an hour to be removed by force), the military moved in, and peace was eventually restored. Allen and several other players were arrested. In court, the judge said that the prisoners had shown remorse, and that 'the length of time this custom has prevailed might be some extenuation'. He let Allen and the others off with a suspended sentence and a fine, but reiterated that the ban must remain: 'However innocent the play might anciently have been, from the increased size of the town and the present state of society, it is impossible to permit it to be continued any longer, and the laws and authorities must be supported.' Football was banned in Derby, and was also suppressed in nearby Ashbourne. The *Mercury* rejoiced, calling the game 'a vestige of a semi barbarous age' and a 'reproach upon civilisation'.

ARCTIC CONDITIONS

In 1850, a game of football was played inside the Arctic Circle between the crew of British survey ship the HMS Herald and a group of natives. The crew encountered the natives (most likely Inuipat Eskimos) near Wainwright's Inlet on the north slope of Alaska. Approaching slowly in canoes, the natives held up their hands to signal friendship. The crew followed the natives ashore, and gifts of tobacco and beads were traded for sealskin boots, ivory tools and reindeer meat. 'They danced and sang for our amusement,' recorded the ship's captain, Henry Kellet, 'and played football with the seamen (who had not a chance with them).' If the natives were well-practised, that is most likely because Eskimos have been playing their own version of football since medieval times. Called *akraurak*, the game is played with a stitched hide ball filled with seeds or moss. Two even-numbered teams attempt to drive the ball through their opponents' goal, which is marked out in the snow.

STRANGE REVEL

A curious game of football took place at the annual Windsor Revel in August 1840. The four-a-side game involved players having 'their legs tied 15 inches apart, and their hands confined'. According to the *Era* newspaper, the winners were presented with a cheese.

WEDDING KICK

A strange football-related wedding ritual was related by *Notes and Queries* magazine in October 1857: 'I have heard of a custom of a football being placed before the bride on leaving the church, which the husband orders her to kick, and so makes her immediately commence her obedience to him.'

PUBLIC SCHOOL GAMES

The codification of football began in England's public schools, where pupils took the mob game and shaped it to meet their needs. Not all of the schools had playing fields, and in many cases the type of football played was dictated by the playing area that was available. The end result was that each school had a different set of rules, which made playing matches between different institutions somewhat complicated.

Charterhouse: The confined space of the original school's cloisters made the mob game impossible. Instead, pupils developed a new and influential kicking and dribbling game, incorporating forward passing and an early offside rule.

Eton: Two types of football were played at Eton – the Wall Game and the Field Game. The latter, which didn't allow handling of the ball, was a clear predecessor of association football. The Field Game rules were first recorded in 1847.

Harrow: This game used 'bases' rather than goals, but was otherwise similar to early association football. Players could take catches, but couldn't run with the ball in their hands.

Rugby: The Rugby game allowed players to run with the ball in hand, allegedly following the example of former pupil William Webb Ellis, making it distinct from other forms of football. The first written rules were established in 1845.

Westminster: A particularly rough dribbling game, this version allowed players to catch the ball and then kick it out of their hands, but again outlawed running with the ball.

Winchester: This complicated dribbling game involved a human 'goal', with points scored for kicking the ball over his head. The pitch was marked off with rope, and surrounded by a horde of 'kickers-in' – essentially public school ball boys.

Football at Charterhouse, 1858

UNIVERSITY GAMES

As public school pupils moved on to university they inevitably took their games with them, in all their variations. University footballers were forced to draw up new rules, which necessarily were hybrids of those from the schools – although it was not always possible to agree to compromise.

Cambridge: Arguably the most influential set of early football rules, these were first drawn up in 1848. Catching the ball was allowed, but running with it was not. Tripping, pushing and holding were outlawed. The game was closely related to the Eton Field Game, probably because the majority of members of the Cambridge football committee were Eton old boys. An updated version of the Cambridge rules, drawn up in 1863, was used as a template for the FA's Laws of the Game.

Oxford: It seems to have been more difficult to come up with an agreeable set of rules at Oxford. Instead, inter-varsity matches would be played between old boys from specific schools by their old school rules. For example, Oxford-based Eton old boys would play Cambridge-based Eton old boys at the Eton Field Game. Oxford would also play other universities using Harrow, Rugby and Winchester football rules.

CAMBRIDGE RULES

Although first drawn up in 1848, the earliest surviving set of rules for the Cambridge football game are these from 1856:

1. This club shall be called the UNIVERSITY FOOT BALL CLUB.

2. At the commencement of the play, the ball shall be kicked off from the middle of the ground: after every goal there shall be a kick-off in the same way.

3. After a goal, the losing side shall kick off; the sides changing goals, unless a previous arrangement be made to the contrary.

4. The ball is out when it has passed the line of the flag-posts on either side of the ground, in which case it shall be thrown in straight.

5. The ball is behind when it has passed the goal on either side of it.

6. When the ball is behind it shall be brought forward at the place where it left the ground, not more than 10 paces, and kicked off.

7. Goal is when the ball is kicked through the flag-posts and under the string.

8. When a player catches the ball directly from the foot, he may kick it as he can without running with it. In no other case may the ball be touched with the hands, except to stop it.

9. If the ball has passed a player, and has come from the direction of his own goal, he may not touch it till the other side have kicked it, unless there are more than three of the other side before him. No player is allowed to loiter between the ball and the adversaries' goal.

10. In no case is holding a player, pushing with the hands, or tripping up allowed. Any player may prevent another from getting to the ball by any means consistent with the above rules.

11. Every match shall be decided by a majority of goals.

FOOTBALL WITH A SKULL

In Berwick in 1857, a group of boys were apprehended after being seen playing football in the town with a human skull. Inquiries led to a young girl, who claimed to have found 'a quantity of human bones' in the street. She had hidden the bones in the hope of selling them, only for the skull to be uncovered by the boys. According to the *Liverpool Mercury*, the bones were found to belong to 'a gentleman of the town, but how they came to be thrown into the streets has not transpired'.

FRENCH FANCY

In June 1858, an unusual football match was played in Biarritz between five Frenchmen and five Spanish Basques. 'The manner in which the game is played differs altogether from that seen in England,' reported the *Birmingham Daily Post*, 'the players stationing themselves in a wide open piece of ground marked with lines, over which the ball must be struck by each party alternately, until one fails, which has the effect of putting them out.' The French won the match, and were awarded a prize of 2,000 francs.

MOORISH SLIPPERS

Soldiers accompanying the Moorish ambassador from Morocco caused great amusement when they played football during a trip to England in 1860. Accommodated at William Claridge's private farm in Hendon, the soldiers enjoyed a boisterous game – although their footwear may not have been entirely suitable. 'Sometimes, after a violent kick,' the *Birmingham Daily Post* reported, 'their slippers would accompany the ball.'

REFEREE!

In 1841, one of the first recorded club matches took place between the Body-Guards Club from Rochdale and their local rivals the Fear-Noughts Club, with a cash prize and a barrel of gin up for grabs. Understandably, with so much at stake, the teams had to ensure a fair result. It was decided that each side should appoint an umpire. This had a direct bearing on the result. With the game level, the Body-Guards brought a by-stander not connected with the game onto the field to play for them. The Body-Guards' own umpire decided that this was foul play, and awarded the game – and the prizes – to the Fear-Noughts. Referees or umpires became more common in the years that followed. At a match in Cheltenham in 1849 there were two officials on the ground and another 'in trib-une' (most likely arbitrating from an elevated viewpoint). The written rules of the Eton Field Game from 1847 make specific mention of a referee: 'To prevent dispute it is better to ap-point, before the game begins, two umpires, one chosen by each party, and a referee to be agreed on by both parties, whose decision, if the umpires differ, is to be final.' Referees weren't included in the Football Association's Laws of the Game when they were drawn up in 1863. However, by the 1870s it was common for association matches to be officiated by two umpires and a referee. Initially, the officials waved handkerchiefs to grab players' attention, but by the mid-1870s pea whistles had become common. It wasn't until 1891 that the referee was finally included in the Laws of the Game, and moved onto the playing field, with the umpires shifted to the sidelines, becoming linesmen. The first three FA Cup finals were refereed by civil servant Alfred Stair, who also played for the Upton Park Club. Other notable referees of the Victorian era include the formidable Francis Marindin of Royal Engineers, and influential football innovator CW Alcock of Wanderers. The referee at the 1878 FA Cup final was Upton Park's Segar Bastard, a racehorse-owning solicitor, who also refereed the first England versus Wales international.

FA CUP FINAL REFEREES

Year	Referee
1872	Alfred Stair (London)
1873	Alfred Stair (London)
1874	Alfred Stair (London)
1875	CW Alcock (London)
1876	William Rawson (Oxford)
1877	Sidney Havill Wright (Great Marlow)
1878	Segar Bastard (London)
1879	CW Alcock (London)
1880	Francis Marindin (London)
1881	William Pierce Dix (Sheffield)
1882	Charles Clegg (Sheffield)
1883	Francis Marindin (London)
1884	Francis Marindin (London)
1885	Francis Marindin (London)
1886	Francis Marindin (London)
1887	Francis Marindin (London)
1888	Francis Marindin (London)
1889	Francis Marindin (London)
1890	Francis Marindin (London)
1891	Charles Hughes (Northwich)
1892	Charles Clegg (Sheffield)
1893	Charles Hughes (Northwich)
1894	Charles Hughes (Northwich)
1895	John Lewis (Blackburn)
1896	William Simpson (Derby)
1897	John Lewis (Blackburn)
1898	John Lewis (Blackburn)
1899	Aaron Scragg (Crewe)
1900	Arthur Kingscott (Derby)

SHEFFIELD FC

Officially regarded as the oldest football club in the world, Sheffield FC was founded in 1857 – and still exists today. Formed by Nathaniel Creswick and William Prest, the club's inaugural meeting was held on 24 October 1857 at Parkfield House in the Highfield district of the town. Although based in a northern industrial town, Sheffield FC wasn't a working class club. Creswick (a solicitor) and Prest (a wine merchant) were both well-to-do men, and their club was one for the gentry. It's thought that Creswick and Prest – both keen sportsmen – wrote to public schools requesting copies of their rulebooks, and used them as a basis from which to create their own Sheffield Rules, first published in 1858. Prest's brother attended Eton and Cambridge, and his influence may have played a part in the fact that Sheffield football closely resembled the Eton field and Cambridge games. Catching was allowed, but running with the ball in hand was not. Tripping and hacking were banned. Later drafts of the rules included the rouge – an alternative scoring method pioneered at Eton. Free-kicks and corner-kicks were among the innovations introduced as the rules evolved. As the only football club in existence, it was difficult to find opponents. Instead, Sheffield FC arranged matches between its own members, dividing teams using billings such as 'Marrieds vs Singles'. Then, in 1860, Hallam FC was formed, and the local rivals were able to play each other in what has become known as the 'Rules Derby'. By the mid 1860s there was a thriving local football scene, with Sheffield at the heart of it. The club's Harry Waters Chambers attended the first meeting of the Football Association in 1863 as an observer, and within a few weeks Sheffield FC had become the FA's first northern member. However, Sheffield didn't adopt the FA's Laws of the Game, and continued to play by their own rules, while attempting to get the FA's rules changed. Several compromises were made, and Sheffield finally adopted the 'London' rules in 1878.

Sheffield FC, 1857

CLUB VERSUS CLUB

The first ever inter-club football match took place on Boxing Day in 1860, between Hallam FC and Sheffield FC. The pitch was covered in snow, but the *Sheffield Daily Telegraph* reported 'a large number of spectators' who were 'extremely liberal with their plaudits' ('and equally unsparing with their sarcasm'). 'The day was beautiful, and the uniform of the men contrasting with each other and the pure snow had a most picturesque appearance,' the paper observed. Sheffield played in 'their usual scarlet and white garments', indicating that the club had a regular kit. Players slid around on the pitch, but no accidents were reported. 'It would be invidious to pick out the play of any particular gentleman when all did well,' said the *Telegraph*, 'but we must give the palm to the Sheffield players as being the most scientific and also the most alive to the advantage of upsetting the opponent.' By the time darkness brought an end to proceedings, Sheffield had won 2-0 'and went home fully satisfied with their victory'.

SHEFFIELD RULES

This is the influential set of rules drawn up by Sheffield FC's Nathaniel Creswick and William Prest in 1858. Notable are the 'Fair Catch' rule, and the ability to charge and push, but not hack or trip. Rule 8 allows pushing and hitting of the ball with the hand, although holding the ball – as practiced at Rugby – is outlawed. This rule was amended in subsequent drafts to remove the ability to push and hit the ball. Later versions of the rules introduced rouges – an additional method of point scoring designed to reduce the number of drawn matches and previously found in the Eton Field Game.

1. The kick-off from the middle must be a place-kick.

2. Kick out must not be more than 25 yards out of goal.

3. Fair Catch is a catch from any player provided the ball has not touched the ground or has not been thrown from touch and is entitled to a free-kick.

4. Charging is fair in case of a place-kick (with the exception of a kick-off as soon as a player offers to kick) but he may always draw back unless he has actually touched the ball with his foot.

5. Pushing with the hands is allowed but no hacking or tripping up is fair under any circumstances whatever.

6. No player may be held or pulled over.

7. It is not lawful to take the ball off the ground (except in touch) for any purpose whatever.

8. The ball may be pushed or hit with the hand, but holding the ball except in the case of a free-kick is altogether disallowed.

9. A goal must be kicked but not from touch nor by a free-kick from a catch.

10. A ball in touch is dead, consequently the side that touches it down must bring it to the edge of the touch and throw it straight out from touch.

11. Each player must provide himself with a red and dark blue flannel cap, one colour to be worn by each side.

FIRST FOOTBALL CLUBS

c.1841: The Body-Guards, the Fear-Noughts (both Rochdale)
1848: The Early Risers (Newcastle upon Tyne)
1849: Surrey FC
1857: Sheffield FC
1859: Wanderers
1860: Hallam FC
1861: Crystal Palace (original)
1862: Notts County
1863: Royal Engineers, Stoke City
1864: Wrexham
1865: Nottingham Forest
1866: Upton Park FC
1867: Queen's Park, Sheffield Wednesday
1869: Clapham Rovers
1870: Darwen, Rotherham United
1871: Old Etonians, Reading
1872: Clydesdale, Kettering Town, Rangers, Renton, Telford
1873: Colchester United
1874: Aston Villa, Hearts, Macclesfield, Northwich Victoria
1875: Birmingham City, Blackburn Rovers, Hibernian
1876: Falkirk, Middlesbrough, Partick Thistle, Port Vale
1877: Blackpool, Bolton, Clyde, Crewe Alexandra, Wolves
1878: Everton, Grimsby, Ipswich, Man United, West Brom
1879: Doncaster Rovers, Fulham, Sunderland, Swindon Town
1880: Kidderminster Harriers, Manchester City
1881: Leyton Orient, Newcastle United, Preston, Watford
1882: Barnet, Burnley, QPR, Tottenham Hotspur
1883: Bristol Rovers, Coventry City, Darlington, Stockport
1884: Derby County, Leicester, Lincoln, Tranmere Rovers
1885: Bury, Luton Town, Millwall, Southampton
1886: Arsenal, Plymouth Argyle, Shrewsbury Town
1887: Barnsley, Cheltenham Town, Wycombe Wanderers
1888: Celtic, Walsall
1889: Bath, Brentford, Forest Green Rovers, Sheffield United
1890: AFC Bournemouth

WANDERERS

One of the most important clubs of football's formative years, Wanderers was founded in 1859 as Forest FC by a group of public school old boys, led by brothers John and Charles Alcock – just 18 and 16 at the time. Both had been educated at Harrow, and the club adopted that school's style of play. Charles (the influential football figure better known as CW) later described Forest as 'the first club to work on a definite basis with the distinct object of circulating and popularising the game'. The Alcocks lived in Chingford, and Forest played in nearby Leytonstone. Initial games were played between members, before the club's first match against external opposition, on 15 March 1862, when Forest beat the original Crystal Palace 1-0. From that starting point, the club looked pretty much unstoppable. Records show that the team played nine games in 1863, and won all of them, scoring 30 goals and conceding just one. The Alcocks were the star men, with Charles in particular forging a reputation as a fearsome goal-scorer. It was John though, as club captain, who represented founding member Forest at the inaugural meeting of the Football Association in 1863. In the following year, Forest began to move away from their Leytonstone ground and play games as the Wanderers. The new name stuck, although Wanderers eventually stopped wandering and settled at Kennington Oval. The arrival of football's first major competition brought major success. Wanderers won the inaugural FA Cup final in 1872, beating Royal Engineers 1-0, and went on to win the cup five times within the competition's first seven years, with players like Arthur Kinnaird and Charles Wollaston playing prominent roles. However, a rapid decline followed. With so many rival teams around, it became difficult for the old-stagers to raise a team. Ironically, the club formed to promote football was undone by the game's popularity. By 1881, Wanderers were reduced to playing annual exhibition matches. The club folded in 1884, although it has since been revived in a modern incarnation that formed in 2009.

Forest FC, 1863 (Alcock brothers in centre)

FOREST FC / CW ALCOCK RECORD 1863-64

Date	Opposition	Score	CW Alcock
21/02/1863	Barnes	1-0	One goal
14/03/1863	Barnes	1-0	One goal
21/03/1863	Crystal Palace	2-1	Two goals
07/11/1863	Richmond	3-0	Didn't score
14/11/1863	Barnes	5-0	Two goals
21/11/1863	Richmond	5-0	One goal
28/11/1863	NN Club	4-0	Didn't score
12/12/1863	Barnes	1-0	Scorer unknown
19/12/1863	Thompson's XI	4-0	One goal
23/01/1864	King's College	2-1	Didn't score
06/02/1864	Harrow School	0-0	No scorer
13/02/1864	Thompson's XI	2-2	One goal
27/02/1864	NN Club	0-0	No scorer
19/11/1864	Crystal Palace	1-0	One goal
26/11/1864	Civil Service FC	1-0	Didn't score

'SOCCER'

It's something of a myth that Victorians commonly referred to association football as 'soccer'. The practice was originally pretty much confined to Oxford University, where students thought it was terribly amusing to suffix abbreviations of almost every word with '-er'. So football was 'footer' and rugby was 'rugger', and association football became contracted and suffixed to become 'soccer' (or 'socker'), apparently on the instigation of future England captain Charles Wreford-Brown around 1886. The word 'soccer' was rarely used elsewhere, with the first recorded use not occurring until 1895. Instead, newspapers referred to 'the association game', until rugby became suitably separated, after which the round ball game was plain old 'football'.

A TOUCH OF ROUGE

Early Victorian football matches weren't just decided by goals – teams could also win by scoring rouges. Derived from public school games (particularly the Eton Field Game), a rouge is probably best described as a cross between a corner-kick and a rugby try. It was included in the Sheffield Rules from around 1860 in an effort to reduce the number of drawn games. A rouge was obtained when the ball was kicked wide of the goalposts and touched down by the attacking team. A goal outweighed any number of rouges, and it was only where a match finished level on goals that it would be decided on rouges. An example of how the rouge worked in the context of a match is contained in an 1866 match report from the *Times*: 'Five minutes before the conclusion of the match Oxford got a rouge, but Cambridge remained the winners by one goal to one rouge.' The Sheffield FA attempted to get the Football Association to introduce rouges into the Laws of the Game, without success. Sheffield abolished the rouge in 1868, replacing it with goal-kicks and corner-kicks.

RULES DEBATE

The problem of clubs, schools and other institutions not being able to play each other at football due to incompatible sets of rules came to a head in the early 1860s, when a series of debates appeared in newspaper correspondence columns. Fred Lillywhite, the sports retailer, had already written to *Bell's Life in London* in 1859, stating his intention to publish a guide to the laws of football: 'If Eton and Rugby, and the other schools and colleges, would form themselves into a committee and arrange that one code of laws could be acknowledged throughout the world, it would be a great benefit to all.' However, it wasn't until 1861 that representatives of the schools, writing under pseudonyms such as 'A Westminster' and 'An Old Rugbean', began to seriously discuss the issue via the pages of publications such as *Bell's*, the *Sporting Gazette*, and the *Field*. One unnamed correspondent to the *Field* wrote, 'It is found impossible to get up a game, and, unless the public schools will combine and draw up a code of rules under which football can be played by all classes, we despair of seeing it take the place which it deserves to occupy as a national winter amusement.' Two weeks later, former Cambridge man JC Thring supplied a letter entitled 'Football, Simple and Universal', in which he criticised the schools' reluctance to adopt a common set of rules. In particular, Thring blamed followers of the Rugby code for refusing to compromise, and called their game 'thoroughly un-English and barbarous'. Thring and like-minded correspondents JD Cartwright and 'A Lover of Football' wrote a series of influential letters and articles that attempted to find common ground between the various existing sets of rules in order to settle upon one unified code. By 1863, the debate had reached the letters pages of the *Times*, with the likes of 'Etonensis', 'Harroviensis' and 'Rugbaeensis' arguing the merits of their own particular rulebooks. Such was the difference of opinion that the debate continued well beyond the event that was intended to settle it – the formation of the Football Association.

THE SIMPLEST GAME

Known to his friends as Charles, JC Thring was one of the most influential figures in the creation of the rules of football. His love of football was developed at Shrewsbury School, and in 1848, while studying at King's College, Charles and his friend Henry de Witton led the initiative to draw up the Cambridge Rules. Later revisions of those rules were used as a template for the FA's Rules of the Game. By 1861, Charles was working as an assistant master at Uppingham School, where his elder brother Edward was headmaster. Charles became heavily involved in the football rules debate in newspaper letters columns, and drew up his own set of rules, which he called 'The Simplest Game'. He published those rules alongside a 'more elaborate' set called 'The Second Game' in a pamphlet, *The Winter Game*, in 1862. The pamphlet also contained a section entitled 'Advice to Players'. 'If you get shinned, either accidentally (which will happen with the best player) or by a clumsy tyro,' he wrote, 'use cold water applications, with dilution of arnica, and forget it as soon as possible.' On rules, he expressed disdain for the Rugby game, which he said 'has unhappily been adopted by many clubs, who, if they had any other well-known codes to choose from, would probably have given to them the decided preference'. It was not Charles' intention to persuade the institutions to ditch their own rules completely, but rather to provide them with the option of a universal code to be used when required. Unfortunately, his rules were all but ignored by the universities and schools he was targeting. Instead Charles shifted his attention to the group of football clubs that formed the Football Association, and by the end of 1863 Uppingham School was a member of the FA. However, Charles had apparently signed the school up without the knowledge of Edward. Uppingham's membership was short-lived, and it seems that Charles and Edward may have fallen out. Charles left Uppingham in 1864 and joined the clergy. He had no further recorded involvement in football, and died in 1909.

FORGOTTEN MAN

John Dyer (or JD) Cartwright played an important – if largely forgotten – role in the development of association football. However, his tragic early death prevented him from seeing the game take off. A much-admired young journalist and poet, JD Cartwright wrote for publications including the *Era*, the *Lady* and the *Field*. It was for the latter, in early 1863, that he wrote a series of detailed articles documenting and examining the various sets of football rules that existed at the time. He was a football enthusiast, and his articles revealed that he favoured the kicking and passing game played at the likes of Charterhouse and Cambridge. Cartwright's research and writing clearly set out the many differences – and similarities – in football rules, and highlighted ways in which they could be brought together to create one universal code. His articles were undeniably influential. However, by the time the Football Association drew up its Laws of the Game, Cartwright had been struck by illness. In the summer of 1864, having been 'for some time in a delicate state of health', he travelled to Bristol to visit his sister. While there, he drowned at the local swimming baths. 'His future career was most promising,' reported the *Era*, 'and his sudden distressing death has caused much grief to his family, as well as to numerous friends, who regarded him not only for his great talent, but for his amiable disposition, unassuming manners and gentlemanly behaviour.' He was just 25 years old.

ORIGINAL LIVERPOOL FC

The original Liverpool Football Club was founded in 1857 by a group of old boys from Rugby School. But this wasn't the Liverpool FC we know today. Favouring the Rugby rules, this became one of the first ever rugby clubs. Having merged with St Helens RUFC, it's now much better known as Liverpool St Helens. The other Liverpool FC, meanwhile, formed in 1892.

CW ALCOCK

Charles William Alcock was one of the first great footballers and an incredibly influential administrator. Born in Sunderland in 1842, Alcock moved to Chingford as a child, and studied at Harrow. In 1859, still a teenager, he formed the Forest football club with his older brother John. Forest quickly became one of the best teams in the area, with young goalscorer 'Charlie' the best player. He was closely involved alongside John as Forest (later renamed Wanderers) became a founding member of the FA. CW Alcock joined the committee in 1866, and was appointed FA secretary in 1870. His first big innovation was the creation of the FA Cup competition in 1871. Alcock was still playing, and, almost inevitably, he won the FA Cup in its first season, as captain of Wanderers. He had also been busy organising a series of representative matches (later known as the Alcock Internationals) between London-based Scottish and English players, and in 1872 he arranged the first official international match between Scotland and England. Alcock had been due to play in the match, but injury forced him to act as umpire. He did captain England in a subsequent match against Scotland in 1875 – and scored in a 2-2 draw. A keen cricketer, Alcock also worked as an administrator and innovator in that sport – he arranged the first Test Match between England and Australia in 1880. He was a journalist by trade, and wrote about sport for various publications, including the *Field* and the *Sportsman*, and his own *Football Annuals*, which he published from 1868. His writing encouraged the uptake and development of football as 'one universal game', and set out innovative tactical ideas involving teamwork and passing. Ever the moderniser, in 1885 he proposed the legalisation of professionalism, which would change football forever. Alcock served as FA secretary until 1895, and died in Brighton in 1907, aged 64. A blue plaque now marks his birthplace at 10 Norfolk Street, Sunderland. His influence on the early game makes him arguably the most important individual in the history of football.

CW Alcock, 1895

ORIGINAL CLUB NAMES

Arsenal: Dial Square (1886)
Barnet: Woodville FC (1882)
Barnsley: Barnsley St Peter's (1887)
Birmingham City: Small Heath Alliance (1875)
Blackpool: Victoria FC (1877)
Bolton Wanderers: Christ Church FC (1874)
AFC Bournemouth: Boscombe St John's (1890)
Bristol Rovers: The Black Arabs (1882)
Cardiff City: Riverside FC (1899)
Colchester United: Colchester Town (1873)
Coventry City: Singers FC (1883)
Everton: St Domingo's FC (1878)
Fulham: Fulham St Andrew's Church Sunday School FC (1879)
Gillingham: New Brompton (1893)
Grimsby Town: Grimsby Pelham (1878)
Leicester City: Leicester Fosse (1884)
Leyton Orient: Eagle Cricket Club (1886)
Liverpool: Everton FC and Athletic Grounds Ltd (1892)
Manchester City: West Gorton St Mark's (1880)
Manchester United: Newton Heath LYR FC (1878)
Newcastle United: Stanley FC (1881)
Oldham Athletic: Pine Villa (1895)
Oxford United: Headington United (1893)
Rotherham United: Thornhill FC (1870)
Sheffield Wednesday: The Wednesday (1867)
Southampton: St Mary's Young Men's Association FC (1885)
Stockport County: Heaton Norris Rovers (1883)
Stoke City: Stoke Ramblers (1863)
Sunderland: Sunderland and District Teachers AFC (1879)
Tottenham Hotspur: Hotspur FC (1882)
Tranmere Rovers: Belmont FC (1884)
West Bromwich Albion: West Bromwich Strollers (1878)
West Ham United: Thames Ironworks FC (1895)
Wolverhampton Wanderers: St Luke's FC (1877)
Yeovil Town: Yeovil Casuals (1895)

UGLY MATCH

At Westminster school in November 1856, a football match was played that was billed as 'Handsome vs Ugly'. It was 'a fine game', apparently, and the Ugly XI won 3-2. 'Luckily for Ugly,' reported *Bell's Life*, 'this match was played in fog.

LUNATIC FOOTBALL

Attempts to improve circumstances for patients at lunatic asylums in Victorian times often involved the arrangement of football games. Newspapers contain numerous accounts of outings to play football, including a very agreeable-sounding 'picnic party' from the Sussex Lunatic Asylum in 1862, which involved football, pies, and 'plenty of homebrewed beer'.

SWISS ROLE

The Lausanne Football and Cricket Club was founded by British students in Switzerland in 1860, and is regarded as the first football club in continental Europe. The club became a founding member of the Swiss Football Association in 1895. Then, in 1897, Lausanne reached the final of the Swiss Serie A competition. However, its British players refused to play the final on a Sunday, and the club was disqualified.

MEETING OF CAPTAINS

The following advertisement appeared in the sporting press in October 1863: 'FOOTBALL: A MEETING will be HELD at the Freemasons' Tavern, Queen-street, Lincoln's Inn on Monday the 26th instant, at 7 o'clock, pm, for the purpose of promoting the adoption of a general code of rules for football, when the captains of all clubs are requested to attend.'

FOOTBALL ASSOCIATION

On Monday 26 October 1863, a meeting took place at the Freemasons' Tavern in London 'for the purpose of forming an association with the object of establishing a definite code of rules for the regulation of football'. The meeting was arranged by Ebenezer Cobb Morley, the captain of Barnes FC, following a long-running exchange of correspondence conducted by interested parties via newspaper letter columns. 13 clubs were represented at the meeting, including Morley's Barnes, John and Charles Alcock's Forest, and the original Crystal Palace club (formed in 1861 and dissolved in 1876). Arthur Pember of the NN (No Names) Club was appointed president of the new Football Association, and Morley was appointed secretary. 11 of the clubs represented at the meeting agreed to become founder members, paying an annual subscription fee of one pound and one shilling. Charterhouse School and Bucks FC (from High Wycombe) declined to join. Charterhouse was represented by Bertram Fulke Hartshorne, who stated that, while he thought it desirable that a common code of rules be adopted, he couldn't agree to become a member unless the other public schools also agreed to join. Letters of invite were sent to the prominent schools, but only JC Thring's Uppingham agreed to join. Neither president Pember nor secretary Morley were public school educated (Pember worked as a journalist and Morley was a solicitor), and there was clearly an element of division between the public schools and the newly-formed association. However, that meant there was no inter-school rivalry on the committee, and perhaps made it easier to create a definitive set of rules. The FA's Laws of the Game were drafted by Morley and debated over five subsequent meetings. Disagreements over the laws led to several founding members (including Blackheath and Crusaders) resigning before a game had been played. However, other prominent clubs (including Sheffield FC and Royal Engineers) joined the FA before the end of 1863 as association football began to get underway.

FA FOUNDING MEMBERS IN OCTOBER 1863

Barnes FC
Blackheath
Blackheath Proprietary School
Civil Service (War Office) FC
Crusaders (London)
Crystal Palace (1861)
Kensington School
Forest FC (Leytonstone)
NN Club (Kilburn)
Perceval House (Blackheath)
Surbiton FC

DECLINED TO JOIN

Bucks FC (High Wycombe)
Charterhouse
Harrow
Westminster
Eton (did not respond)
Rugby (did not respond)
Winchester (did not respond)

FA MEMBERS IN DECEMBER 1863

Barnes FC
Civil Service (War Office) FC
Crystal Palace (1861)
Forest FC
Forest School
NN Club
Royal Engineers
Sheffield FC
Uppingham School

FIRST ASSOCIATION MATCHES

When, where and between whom was the first association football match played? There are several contenders:

Blackheath 2-0 Perceval House, 31 October 1863
This 'keenly contested' game, with both goals scored by Sinclair, was played at Blackheath just five days after the Football Association was formed. However, the Laws of the Game had yet to be drawn up. Blackheath preferred the rugby code, and both Blackheath and Perceval House would withdraw from the FA before the association rules were finalised.

Forest 1-0 Barnes, 12 December 1863
This game between two of the FA's leading member clubs wasn't played by the new laws. 'There was some talk about the rules, and we regret to say some little temper displayed,' reported *Bell's Life*. 'This shows the good of the new rules drawn up by the FA, for when they have come into universal use, games can be played without dispute.'

Forest 4-0 Thompson's XI, 19 December 1863
After the trouble against Barnes, Forest had resolved to use the association rules for all subsequent matches, 'with the exception of those that are already arranged'. This 'most spirited and exciting' game against a team put together by Messrs A and WJ Thompson fell into the 'already arranged' category, so was almost certainly not an association match.

Barnes 0-0 Richmond, 19 December 1863
This was the first match actually recorded as being played under association rules, despite the fact that Richmond weren't FA members. 'Very little difficulty was experienced on either side in playing the new rules – their simplicity preventing disputes arising,' reported the *Sporting Gazette*. Despite this success, the match was apparently as lacklustre as the scoreline might suggest.

President's Side 2-0 Secretary's Side, 9 January 1864

The first official association football match was an exhibition game between two FA representative teams – the President's Side and the Secretary's Side – both of which fielded 14 players. It took place at Battersea Park, and the likes of Arthur Pember, Ebenezer Cobb Morley, Alexander Morton and Harry Waters Chambers all played. The President's Side won 2-0, with both goals scored by CW Alcock. After the match, the players dined together and raised a toast: 'Success to football, irrespective of class or creed.'

NN 3-0 Barnes, 30 January 1864

This was the first club match played under FA rules between two association members. No Names and Barnes were captained by FA president Arthur Pember and secretary Ebenezer Cobb Morley. *Bell's Life* called for 'a little more alacrity on behalf of the Barnes goalkeepers' but singled out Morley for his 'very pretty play'. Baker (2) and de Pothonier scored the goals in a 15-a-side match, at the NNs' Kilburn ground.

HACKED OFF

The practice of hacking ('kicking an adversary on the front of the leg, below the knee') was considered such an integral part of the Victorian game that there was uproar in 1863 when the newly-formed Football Association discussed plans to ban it. Initial FA rule drafts allowed hacking (and charging, tripping and holding), but subsequent meetings to finalise the rules descended into arguments between 'hackers' and 'non-hackers'. 'Hacking is the true football game,' claimed the Blackheath club's Francis Maule Campbell. Not everyone agreed, though, with key FA instigator Ebenezer Cobb Morley stating, 'If we have hacking, no one will play at football.' Hacking was duly outlawed, prompting several clubs, including Campbell's Blackheath, to quit the Football Association – and form the Rugby Football Union.

NOTTS COUNTY

There are older amateur clubs, but Notts County, founded in 1862, is the oldest professional football club in the world. Originating from Nottinghamshire County Cricket Club, its founders included the famous batsman Richard Daft, his cricketing teammate WA Hodges, and a man whose name suggested he was familiar with the aggressive side of football – Major Hack. The club originally played at the Meadows cricket ground, later moving to Trent Bridge. In its earliest days, County played regular fixtures against that other football old-stager Sheffield FC, often using the Sheffield Rules. The first match between the sides was played in January 1865, in front of 'a good many spectators'. Daft excelled for County, but the more experienced Sheffield won 1-0. By the following year, County had a local rival in the shape of newly-formed Nottingham Forest. The first Nottingham derby was played on 23 March 1866 and ended as a goalless draw – despite the fact that Forest fielded 17 players to County's 11. A rematch in 1867 finished 1-0 to County, with Hodges the scorer. The Nottingham rivalry had some spice about it from the very beginning, with County considering themselves to be a better class of club, made up of 'superior persons' and 'people of importance', while Forest were regarded simply as a 'town club'. County's first great player was Ernest Harwood Greenhalgh, who first appeared for the club in the late 1860s, and was soon appointed captain. The full-back was selected to play for England in the first ever international match, against Scotland in November 1872. County were founder members of the Football League in 1888, but finished second from bottom in its inaugural season. An improvement in form saw the club finish third in the 1890-91 season – and also reach the FA Cup final, only to lose to Blackburn Rovers. They were relegated in 1893, but in the following season became the first second division side to win the FA Cup, beating Bolton Wanderers 4-1 in a game known as 'Logan's Match' due to the hat-trick performance of young Scottish striker Jimmy Logan.

EBENEZER COBB MORLEY

Often referred to as the founder of modern football, Ebenezer Cobb Morley arranged the 1863 meeting of captains that led to the formation of the Football Association. His subsequent enthusiasm did much to establish football as a popular sport. Born in Hull in 1831, Morley moved to London to work as a solicitor in 1858. Not long afterwards he founded the Barnes club, which became a founding member of the FA. Morley was appointed FA secretary at the Association's inaugural meeting, and he subsequently drafted the first Laws of the Game. A fine player, Morley was regularly singled out for individual praise in newspaper reports of Barnes matches. A little older than some of his contemporaries, he captained Barnes into his late 30s, and represented London against Sheffield in 1866. Appointed FA president in 1867, he held the role until 1874. Morley lived a long life, and died in 1924 aged 94. He has rarely been given the recognition his important role in the development of football merits. He is buried in an untended grave in the now-disused Barnes Old Cemetery, and efforts to establish a memorial have been unsuccessful.

LAWS OF THE GAME

First published following the fourth meeting of the Football Association in November 1863:

I. The maximum **length of the ground** shall be 200 yards, the maximum **breadth** shall be 100 yards, the length and breadth shall be marked off with flags; and the **goal** shall be defined by two upright posts, eight yards apart, without any tape or bar across them.

II. The Game shall be commenced by a **place kick** from the centre of the ground by the side winning the toss, the other side shall not approach within 10 yards of the ball until it is kicked off. After a goal is won the losing side shall be entitled to kick off.

III. The two sides shall change goals after each goal is won.

IV. A goal shall be won when the ball passes over the space between the goal posts (at whatever height) not being thrown, knocked on or carried.

V. When the ball is in **touch** the first player who shall touch it shall kick or throw it from the point on the boundary line where it left the ground, in a direction at right angles with the boundary line.

VI. A player shall be **out of play** immediately he is in front of the ball and must return behind the ball as soon as possible. If the ball is kicked past a player by his own side, he shall not touch or kick it or advance until one of the other side has first kicked it or one of his own side on a level with or in front of him, has been able to kick it.

VII. In case the ball goes behind the goal line: if a player on the side to whom the goal belongs first touches the ball, one of his side shall be entitled to a free kick from the goal line at the point opposite the place where the ball shall be touched. If a player of the opposite side first touches the ball, one of his side shall be entitled to a free kick from a point 15 yards outside the goal line, opposite the place where the ball is touched.

VIII. If a player makes a **fair catch** he shall be entitled to a **free kick** provided he claims it by making a mark with his heel at once; and in order to take such kick he may go as far back as he pleases, and no player on the opposite side shall advance beyond his mark until he has kicked.

IX. A player shall be entitled to run with the ball towards his adversaries' goal if he makes a fair catch, or catches the ball on the first bound; but in case of a fair catch, if he makes his mark, he shall not then run.

X. If any player shall run with the ball towards his adversaries' goal, any player on the opposite side shall be at liberty to charge, hold, trip or hack him, or to wrest the ball from him, but no player shall be held and hacked at the same time.

XI. Neither tripping nor hacking shall be allowed, and no player shall use his hands or elbows to hold or push his adversary, except in the case provided for by Law 10.

XII. Any player shall be allowed to charge another, provided they are both in active play. A player shall be allowed to charge if even he is out of play.

XIII. A player shall be allowed to throw the ball or pass it to another if he makes a fair catch, or catches the ball on the first bound.

XIV. No player shall be allowed to wear projecting nails, iron plates or gutta percha [rubber] on the soles or heels of his boots.

DEFINITION OF TERMS – *A Place Kick* is a kick at the ball while it is on the ground in any position which the kicker may choose to place it. – *A Free Kick* is the privilege of kicking the ball, without obstruction, in such a manner as the kicker may see fit. – *A Fair Catch* is when the ball is caught, after it has been kicked, knocked on, or thrown on by an adversary, and before it has touched the ground. – *Hacking* is kicking an adversary on the front of the leg, below the knee. – *Tripping* is throwing an adversary with the use of the legs without the hands. – *Charging* is attacking an adversary with the shoulder, chest or body, without using the hands or legs.

TALE OF THE TAPE

The evolution of the crossbar was a slow one – and its ancestor was the tape. The FA's Laws of the Game initially stated that a goal should be 'two upright posts, eight yards apart, *without* any tape or bar across them'. However, other sets of rules did require a tape or cord to be strung between the two goalposts. In a match between Charterhouse and Crusaders in January 1863, Charterhouse's Kenneth Muir Mackenzie shot just over the tape, and appealed that it should have been a goal. 'Some unfortunate accident had happened to the pegs which tightened the cord,' reported *Bell's Life*, 'so that it was hanging slack, and deviating considerably from the straight line, and would not admit the ball under the required limits.' In 1866, after a peculiar incident in which a goal was scored at Reigate, when the kicker 'raised the ball quite 90 feet in the air between the goal-posts', the FA changed its rules to add the requirement for a tape. Solid crossbars began to be used in the 1870s, but, it wasn't until 1882 that the updated Laws of the Game required every club to provide crossbars.

BASES LOADED

Wanderers were almost invincible in the 1865-66 season, having played 16, won 11, drawn four, and lost just one solitary match. That one loss – to Harrow School – owed much to a couple of mitigating circumstances. Firstly, Wanderers 'did not play their entire strength'. Secondly, the match was played according to Harrow rules, the various complications of which involved the substitution of goals with 'bases'. In fact, a Harrovian 'base' was very similar to an association football goal, with the main difference being that, in order to score a base, the ball had to 'touch one of the opposite side to the kicker previously to passing between the base poles'. To Wanderers' credit, they soon mastered the Harrow game, and won a return match by two bases.

DRIBBLING

Dribbling was a key feature of early football, but it wasn't quite the celebrated skill it would become in later years. With passing virtually unheard of, dribbling was pretty much the only way to get the ball from one end of the pitch to the other. However, at a time of limited tactics and formations, there was little room for a cultured dribbler. Much of the early game involved mass 'scrimmages', with the aim of 'driving' the ball towards the opponents' goal. Loose balls could be pounced upon by the fleet-of-foot, but their dribbles were often cut short by hacks and fouls. As tactics developed, football came to embrace dribbling, which, as the *Penny Illustrated* remarked, 'infants and footballites alike are prone to'.

Dribbling at football, Penny Illustrated, 1874

Queen's Park is Scotland's oldest association football club, and one of the most important in the history of the game. Formed in 1867 by a group of men who met to play sports at the Queen's Park Recreation Ground in south Glasgow, the club adopted the motto '*Ludere causa ludendi*' ('Play for the sake of playing'), and remains resolutely amateur to this day. The club quickly became the biggest and best club in Scotland – chiefly due to tight organisation and regimented practice. Incredibly, the club didn't concede a goal in its first eight years of existence. The Scottish football writer David Drummond Bone called Queen's Park Scotland's 'parent club', and described how its growing popularity created a 'football wave', with hundreds of new clubs forming in its wake. But Queen's Park's influence spread beyond Scotland. The club's utilisation of a highly successful 'scientific' passing (or 'combination') game had a pioneering effect on how football would be played in subsequent years. The club joined the English Football Association in 1870, and became the first and only Scottish team to participate in the FA Cup. In 1872, Queen's Park reached the FA Cup semi-final without having to play a match, being awarded three consecutive byes. In the semi-final – the club's first ever competitive match – Queen's Park held the mighty Wanderers to a goalless draw at the Oval. A replay was required, but the Scottish club couldn't afford to make another trip to London. Wanderers received a bye (and went on to win the cup). Later that year, Queen's Park were heavily involved in the organisation of the first official Scotland versus England international match. All of the Scottish XI were Queen's Park players, including captain and goalkeeper Robert Gardner, back William Ker, half-back JJ Thompson, and forward Billy MacKinnon. Queen's Park also played a leading role in the formation of the Scottish Football Association in 1873. The club won the Scottish Cup 10 times during the Victorian era, and also continued to participate in the FA Cup, reaching the final twice.

CELEBRITY FOOTBALLERS

Several early footballers had prominent careers away from the game, but the first real celebrity to play the game was William Henry Gladstone, the eldest son of Prime Minister William Ewart Gladstone, and a high-profile politician in his own right as the Liberal MP for Whitby. An Eton old boy and veteran of the Eton Field Game, he switched to association football after leaving school, and unsurprisingly played for Old Etonians. Despite being born in Wales, Gladstone represented Scotland in two of CW Alcock's 'unofficial internationals', in 1870 and 1871. (Another MP, John Wingfield Malcolm, also played in the 1870 match.) A 6ft-plus chap, Gladstone played as a back for the 'Scottish' team. However, his football career was sidetracked by his other interests, and he played only rarely, never figuring in the Old Etonians FA Cup sides. Nevertheless, in 1873, Gladstone was named by *Gentleman's Magazine* as being 'among the many celebrities who continue to practice football long after their school days'.

FOLLOWING LEEDS

In 1864, a Mr HJ Jenkinson set up the Leeds Football Club, for the purpose of arranging morning and evening games in the town. Within a couple of months, the club had 370 members, and numerous 'branch clubs'. 'Anyone of whatever age or class is allowed to join, who will play without roughness and in a gentlemanly manner,' Jenkinson wrote. 'Football has of late not been a popular game, principally on account of the roughness often attending it, but the rules of the Leeds clubs do away with all objectionable practices, and the astonishing success of the club proves that the game, when played properly, is a real favourite with Englishmen.' Association football didn't really take off in Leeds until the 1880s, with the arrival of teams including Hunslet Wesleyans and a new Leeds FC. Leeds United AFC wouldn't be formed until 1919.

LONDON VS SHEFFIELD

Although Sheffield FC were members of the FA, up until 1877 they didn't play by the FA's Laws of the Game. They preferred their own set of rules – as did other clubs in the surrounding area. So there remained a divide between the 'London Rules' and the Sheffield Rules, and the Football Association and Sheffield FC were effectively friendly rivals. In 1866, Sheffield FC secretary William Chesterman wrote to the FA suggesting a match between the two organisations. The challenge was accepted, and it was agreed that the contest would take place at Battersea Park on 31 March 1866. In deference to the home team, the match would be played under London rules. The match was notable for many reasons. The London team was a representative side including captain Arthur Pember of the NN Club, Ebenezer Cobb Morley of Barnes, and CW Alcock and Arthur Kinnaird of Wanderers. London wore white shirts – as the FA's England team would go on to do. The Sheffield team included only Sheffield FC players, including captain Chesterman and Harry Waters Chambers, and featured no players from other local clubs such as Hallam. The match duration was fixed at 90 minutes, and the ball chosen was the Lillywhites No 5. It was the first recorded instance of either being specified – and 90-minute games and the No 5 ball would subsequently become football fundamentals. Oddly, match reports mention 'touch-downs', effectively rouges, presumably appended to the London rules for this match for the benefit of the Sheffield men. Playing in rain and hail, London scored the first goal after 10 minutes, through Morley. Alcock had a strike disallowed for offside, before JM Martin of Crusaders scored a second for London. After the 90 minutes, London had two goals and four touchdowns to Sheffield's nil. 'Sheffield played all through the game with the greatest pluck and determination, but were fairly overmatched,' reported *Bell's Life*. In all, there were 17 matches played between London and Sheffield through to 1876. Sheffield won nine to London's six, and there were two draws.

LINCOLN SHOT

In the earliest years of association football there were three key clubs outside of London – Sheffield FC, Notts County and Lincoln FC. All three preferred the Sheffield Rules to the Laws of the Game, and in 1866 Lincoln quit the FA. A letter was read out at the FA's annual general meeting stating that the club had tried the association rules but didn't like them, and as such were withdrawing their support. Arthur Pember, chairing the meeting, said he was not surprised, as Lincoln favoured 'hacking, throttling, and other violent practices'. Pember added that he personally had a strong objection to his leg being broken during a game of football. This brought a strong response from Lincoln captain Devereux Garnham, who defended his club's preferred rules, writing, 'For six seasons I have played with these same rules and not a broken leg has ever occurred on our ground.' Garnham concluded that it would be better for football if the FA was to 'shift headquarters to Sheffield'. Lincoln FC continued to play by its own rules until 1884, when it was one of three clubs that merged to form Lincoln City.

FOOTBALL TO MANCHESTER

More than a decade before Manchester United or Manchester City were formed, the good men of Sheffield brought association football to the northern 'cottonopolis'. Two matches were played in early 1866 between Sheffield FC and a team known simply as 'Manchester'. The matches were played under Sheffield Rules, which, according to *Bell's Life*, 'the Manchester men were not sufficiently conversant with to make them successful'. Manchester couldn't raise enough players, suffered severe injures (including a dislocated knee-cap), and ultimately lost. They did, however, win a subsequent match played by rugby rules. It would take a while longer for Manchester to fall in love with association football.

FIRST TOURNAMENT

The Youdan Cup, played in Sheffield in early 1867, was the first ever organised football tournament. Sponsored by local theatre owner and philanthropist Thomas Youdan, the tournament was contested by 12 local teams, and comprised two knockout rounds followed by a three-way final involving Hallam FC, Norfolk, and Mackenzie. The finals were played at Bramall Lane in front of 3,000 spectators. Hallam and Norfolk both beat Mackenzie, and faced off against each other in the deciding match. 'The toss for choice of goals was won by Norfolk, who kicked with the wind, but were unable to score,' reported *Bell's Life*. 'After playing half-time, ends were changed, when it was soon evident the Hallamites had the game in their own hands.' The match was played under Sheffield FA rules and, although there were no goals, Hallam scored two rouges to become football's first cup winners. Unfortunately, the cup was not ready in time to be presented to the winners, and Thomas Youdan was unable to attend the final due to illness. The Youdan Cup subsequently disappeared, but resurfaced in 1997, when Hallam FC bought it from a collector for £2,000. Hallam, now playing in English football's lower tiers, still have the historic cup.

PROOF FOR A RESULT

A bewildering match report appeared in *Bell's Life* in October 1863 concerning a match between Crusaders and Westminster School. Crusaders' Walsingham had a goal disallowed after his shot hit the 'goal-string', and the result was in dispute. 'I will only say that both sides played their best,' wrote the correspondent, 'and that the result of the game proves that, trying to prove a result from such a result, is proof that there is no proof for a result, and, therefore, I leave it to the next match to prove a result, and hoping it will result in a proof that the Crusaders are proof against any bad result.'

ARTHUR PEMBER

First FA president Arthur Pember had a remarkable career away from football. The captain of the NN Club, Pember acted as FA president from the Association's first meeting in 1863 until 1867. After that, however, he left football and England behind. Emigrating to the US, he worked as an investigative journalist for the *New York Times*. Known as 'AP, The Amateur Vagabond' due to his ploy of disguising himself as a tramp, he worked undercover in coal mines, prisons and circuses, and exposed corrupt politicians, spirit mediums and peep-show operators. In 1874 he published a collection of his writing, *The Mysteries and Miseries of the Great Metropolis, With Some Adventures in the Country: Being the Disguises and Surprises of a New-York Journalist*. 'I have submitted to many inconveniences and faced dangers while pursuing my adventures,' he wrote, 'but how could I possibly pen sketches from real life had I not been ready to do so?' It's also worth noting that Pember had – even by Victorian standards – a quite remarkable moustache.

FÚTBOL IN ARGENTINA

Football was introduced to Argentina by railway workers from the north of England. The Buenos Aires Football Club, South America's first association football club, was formed in 1867 by a group of young men led by brothers Thomas and James Hogg, from Skelton in York. The first match took place at Palermo on 20 June between club members divided into the Colorados (Reds) and the Blancos (Whites) – with the teams distinguished by coloured caps. 'There were not so many players as had been expected,' reported the local *Standard* newspaper, and it ended up being an eight-a-side match. The Colorados won 4-0, 'chiefly owing to the superior play of the Messrs Hogg'. The match was played according to FA rules, 'with some slight modifications', and there were problems involving players using their hands instead of their feet. 'However,' reported the *Standard*, 'it was remarkable that considering it was the first time the players had assembled together, they all played well.' Nevertheless, the club subsequently bowed to the whims of those members who had preferred to use their hands, and ditched football in favour of rugby. It would take more than 20 years for association football to become popular in Argentina, with interest being revived by another immigrant, Alexander Watson Hutton, a Scottish teacher from Glasgow's Gorbals. Watson Hutton founded the Buenos Aires English High School in 1884, and placed great importance on physical education, teaching the pupils the intricacies of football. In 1893 he founded the Argentine Association Football League (now the Asociación del Fútbol Argentino). Starting out with just five teams, this was the origin of the Argentine league system that still exists – and now contains around 450 teams. Then, in 1898, Watson Hutton founded, via his school, the Alumni Athletic Club, a highly-successful amateur team that won the Argentine championship 10 times. His son, Arnold, played for the Argentine national team in the early 1900s. 'Alejandro' Watson Hutton is now regarded as the father of Argentine football.

SHEFFIELD WEDNESDAY

An offshoot of a cricket club that played at Bramall Lane, Sheffield Wednesday was formed at a meeting at the city's Adelphi Hotel on 4 September 1867. Known as 'the Wednesday' until 1929, the club joined a thriving Sheffield football scene, and won one of the game's earliest tournaments, the Cromwell Cup, in 1868. Charles and William Clegg, two of the most influential characters in Sheffield football, joined the Wednesday in 1870. And in 1876 Wednesday signed Glasgow shipyard worker James Lang, regarded as the first ever professional footballer. The club left Bramall Lane in 1887, moving to the new Olive Grove ground. Wednesday were founder members of the Football Alliance in 1889, and won it in its first season. The club also reached the 1890 FA Cup final, but were thrashed 6-1 by Blackburn Rovers. However, Wednesday won the FA Cup in 1896, beating Wolves 2-1. Fred Spiksley scored both goals for a team captained by Jack Earp.

CROMWELL CUP

The Cromwell Cup, which took place in Sheffield in 1868, is regarded as only the second football tournament ever staged (after the Youdan Cup – also staged in Sheffield). The Cup was sponsored by local theatre manager Oliver Cromwell, who also played football for the Garrick club. There were four participants, all local clubs that had been formed within the previous two years. In the first round (or semi-finals) the Wednesday beat Exchange 4-0, and Garrick beat Wellington 1-0. The final was played at Wednesday's Bramall Lane on 15 February 1878 in front of around 500 spectators. After 90 minutes there were no goals (or rouges), and it was agreed that the sides would play on, with the next score winning the game. 10 minutes into extra time, the Wednesday scored what was effectively the first ever golden goal to win the Cromwell Cup – a trophy that Sheffield Wednesday still has today.

ALCOCK INTERNATIONALS

In January 1870, a notice appeared in the *Field* inviting players to participate in an association football match 'between the leading representatives of the Scotch and English sections'. The match was billed as a 'great International Football Match', although it has not come to be regarded as such. It was the first of five so-called 'Alcock Internationals' – a series of England versus Scotland games organised by FA secretary CW Alcock. The matches aren't considered official international matches, but they were important stepping stones towards establishing proper England versus Scotland fixtures. For the first Alcock match, only one member of the Scottish team, Kenneth Muir Mackenzie, was actually born in Scotland, and all of those selected were London-based. So the 'London Scottish' side was not regarded as being truly representative of Scotland. In fact, all of the 'London Scottish' players had roots that would have qualified them to play for Scotland under modern rules. Nevertheless, Alcock regarded the team as 'counterfeit', and made efforts to improve matters for subsequent matches. He wrote to the *Glasgow Herald*, appealing for Scottish players to represent their country. 'In Scotland, once essentially the land of football, there should still be a spark left of the old fire,' he wrote. The appeal had limited success, however, attracting only one Scottish player, Robert Smith of Queen's Park, who in any case lived in London. Defeat for the Scots in the second match brought derision from north of the border. 'It must not be supposed that the 11 who represented us in their defeat involved our national reputation as athletes,' wrote a correspondent to the *Scotsman*. Alcock responded, pointing out that he had invited Scottish players to participate. 'The fault lies on the heads of the players of the north,' he wrote, 'not on the management who sought the services of all alike impartially.' However, despite further appeals, no Scotland-based players came forward for the subsequent games, and it would be 1872 before an 'official' international match was played.

1. England 1-1 Scotland, 5 March 1870

Scotland, captained by James Kirkpatrick, took the lead against CW Alcock's England team courtesy of a 'lucky long kick' from Robert Crawford, 'in the reprehensible absence of England's goalkeeper'. A crowd of around 500 watched the match at the Kennington Oval, and the goal was met with 'vociferous applause from the canny Scots, who represented no small portion of the spectators'. However, those canny Scots were to be disappointed as England grabbed a last-minute equaliser courtesy of Alfred Baker, following 'one of the finest runs that has ever been witnessed'.

2. England 1-0 Scotland, 19 November 1870

This victory for England ('who appeared more uniformly skilful than their antagonists') was secured by a single goal, created by Alcock and scored by Robert Walker. The efforts of Queen's Park's Robert Smith, who 'proved most useful from first to last', were not enough to save Scotland from defeat.

3. England 1-1 Scotland, 25 February 1871

Scotland, now captained by Arthur Kinnaird, took the lead through Charles Nepean (a distant uncle of the actor Hugh Grant). However, as in the first match, England scored a late equaliser, with Walker getting his second goal in two games.

4. England 2-1 Scotland, 18 November 1871

Clapham Rovers captain Walker scored another two goals in this England victory, securing a reputation as the star player of the Alcock Internationals. Royal Engineers' Henry Renny-Tailyour scored a consolation goal for Scotland.

5. England 1-0 Scotland, 24 February 1872

Sheffield FC's Charles Clegg became the first non-London player to participate in these games, and he scored England's winning goal 'to the immense delight of the English supporters'. However, the match, played in inclement weather, was a disappointment and the 'unofficial' internationals ended.

CRUEL CHARACTER

Robert Crawford was a renowned Victorian footballer and, quite possibly, a genocidal maniac. Born in Jersey in 1852 and educated at Harrow, Crawford somehow represented Scotland in four of CW Alcock's unofficial international matches between 1870 and 1872. He actually scored Scotland's goal, from 'a rather fluky long kick', in the first 'Alcock international'. After changing his surname to Copland-Crawford in deference to a family benefactor, he played for Wanderers against Queen's Park in the 1872 FA Cup semi-final, and also played cricket for the MCC, before embarking on a distinguished military career, in which he was decorated for action in Afghanistan and Egypt. However, by 1889 he had washed up in Sierra Leone, having resigned his military post, divorced his wife, and abandoned his daughter. Now 37, he was employed by the Sierra Leone police to lead a constabulary force against a local warlord called Mackiah. This he did with apparent relish, killing 'warboys', recapturing towns, and punishing collaborators – often in direct contradiction to the orders of the governor of Sierra Leone. Crawford was clearly a loose cannon, and he became increasingly volatile and unpredictable. He exhibited strange behaviour, and complained of hallucinations. He openly stated that he felt he was going out of his mind. In a final loss of reason, he accused a local boy of theft and brutally tortured him. The 17-year-old was flogged, had salt rubbed in his open wounds, and was subjected to a mock execution. He subsequently died. Crawford was charged with murder, and later convicted of manslaughter. Due to a fragile mental state he was repatriated to England, where he was freed to convalesce at home. Crawford's other crimes soon came to light. In 1890, a report was presented to the House of Commons accusing Crawford of 'the slaughter of an indefinite number of people', 'the burning of six or eight towns', and 'punishments inflicted of a cruel character'. Crawford was never tried for these crimes. He continued to struggle with ill health until his death in 1894.

ROYAL ENGINEERS

Representing the British Army 'Sappers', Royal Engineers AFC was formed around 1863, and came to prominence in the late 1860s under the leadership of Francis Marindin and William Merriman, both Army Captains. All of the club's earliest players were officers, and the discipline, comradeship and ingenuity required by their work served them well on the football field. At a time when most clubs employed an individual kick-and-rush philosophy, Engineers played a well-organised passing game that relied on teamwork. Early match reports spoke of Engineers' 'brilliant play', 'irreproachable organisation', and 'better condition and lasting power'. Engineers' pioneering use of what CW Alcock later termed the 'combination game' allowed them to become the great rival of Wanderers. They narrowly lost to Wanderers in the first FA Cup final in 1872. However, they continued to hone the combination game, and won the cup in 1875, beating Old Etonians 2-0 in a replay. 'Individually, we were sometimes up against better players than ourselves, but collectively we felt equal to any club,' wrote Engineers' cup-winning half-back Lieutenant Richard Ruck. 'We were a veritable band of brothers.'

Royal Engineers, 1872 (Marindin at back row centre)

FA CUP

At a meeting of the Football Association in July 1871, the following proposal was made by CW Alcock: 'It is desirable that a Challenge Cup should be established in connection with the Association, for which all clubs belonging to the association should be invited to compete.' Aside from the 'Alcock Internationals', the FA had yet to organise any fixtures, so this was an ambitious undertaking. But it was one that would help the FA to secure its position as the arbitrator of English football, with the FA Cup becoming the most famous and long-running club competition in the world. The key feature of the FA Cup was its knockout format. Although previous football competitions had featured knockout stages, Old Harrovian Alcock took the idea from his school's Cock House Cup, an annual knockout inter-house football competition, in which the last remaining team was named the 'Cock House'. It was agreed that the FA Challenge Cup would begin in the 1871-72 season. The FA had 50 member clubs at the time, but only 15 entered the inaugural tournament. Three additional clubs applied to enter, but withdrew before the competition began, including Switzerland's Lausanne. There was one remaining 'international' entrant – Scotland's Queen's Park. The others were London teams, plus Lincolnshire's Donington School. There was no prize money to tempt entrants, with the FA promising in addition to the cup '11 medals or badges of trifling value'. Detractors felt awarding any prize at all was unworthy of the amateur game. However, a lack of funds caused problems, particularly for teams that couldn't afford travelling expenses. As a result, there were numerous withdrawals and byes. Most notably, Queen's Park couldn't afford to travel from Glasgow to London for their semi-final replay, allowing Wanderers a bye to the final. The FA Cup gradually found increased popularity and participation. 32 clubs entered in 1875-76, and 54 in 1879-80. By the mid-1880s the competition had more than 100 participants drawn from all over the country.

FA CUP ENTRANTS 1871-72

Team	Progression
Harrow School	Withdrew Before First Round
Lausanne	Withdrew Before First Round
Windsor Home Park	Withdrew Before First Round
Barnes	Second Round Replay
Civil Service	First Round
Clapham Rovers	Second Round
Crystal Palace (1861)	Semi-Final Replay
Donington School	Second Round (Withdrew)
Hampstead Heathens	Quarter-Final
Harrow Chequers	First Round (Withdrew)
Hitchin	Second Round
Marlow	First Round
Maidenhead	Second Round
Queen's Park	Semi-Final Replay (Withdrew)
Reigate Priory	First Round (Withdrew)
Royal Engineers	Final
Upton Park	First Round
Wanderers	Champions

FIRST FA CUP GOAL

The first recorded FA Cup goal was scored on 11 November 1871 by Jarvis Kenrick of Clapham Rovers in a 3-0 away win at Upton Park's West Ham Park ground. Kenrick actually scored twice in the match, played two days before his 19th birthday. A crowd of around 1,500 saw the feat. Clapham, formed in 1869, would go on to win the FA Cup in 1880. But, in its first season, they lost to Wanderers in the second round. Kenrick, also a cricketer who played for Surrey CCC, later joined Wanderers, and won the FA Cup twice with his new club, in 1877 and 1878. He scored two goals in the 1878 final. Despite his goalscoring prowess, Kenrick never played for England.

FIRST FA CUP FINAL

On 16 March 1872, at Kennington Oval, Wanderers and Royal Engineers contested the first ever Football Association Challenge Cup final. 15 clubs entered the inaugural competition but, due to a series of withdrawals and byes, Wanderers were only required to beat Clapham Rovers in order to reach the final. Royal Engineers beat Hitchin, Hampstead Heathens and Crystal Palace on the way to the Oval. The Wanderers team, captained by FA secretary and FA Cup instigator CW Alcock, included some of the greatest footballers of the Victorian era, such as future England captain Charles Wollaston, goalkeeper Reginald Courtenay Welch, and the ubiquitous Alcock. The Royal Engineers team included club captain and full-back Captain Francis Marindin, goalkeeper Captain William Merriman, and soon-to-be Scottish international forward Lieutenant Henry Renny-Tailyour. 2,000 spectators, 'including many ladies', watched the match, which kicked off at the now-traditional 3pm. Royal Engineers, noted for their development of the 'combination' passing game, were regarded as favourites, but they suffered an early blow when Lieutenant Edmund Cresswell broke his collarbone. ('Notwithstanding, he maintained his post until the finish of the game,' reported *Bell's Life*.) Wanderers, with the wind at their backs, had the best of the early play, and scored after 15 minutes, when Robert Vidal dribbled from the halfway line, and set up Morton Betts to finish from a tight angle. Betts was named on the teamsheet and in newspaper reports as 'AH Chequer', derived from the fact that he was also a Harrow Chequers football club member. The teams swapped ends after the goal – as was customary in the 1870s – and, despite now playing into the wind, Wanderers continued to dominate, forcing the Engineers' Captain Merriman into a series of saves. There were no further goals, however, and Wanderers won by a single goal. The *Field* reported that the Wanderers team had displayed, 'some of the best play, individually and collectively, that has ever been shown in an Association game'.

Wanderers 1–0 Royal Engineers
16 March 1872
Kennington Oval, London
Scorer: Betts (15 mins)

Wanderers (1-1-8)

Reginald Courtenay Welch Goalkeeper
Edgar Lubbock Full-Back
Albert Thompson Half-Back
CW Alcock (*Captain*) Forward
Edward Bowen Forward
Alexander Bonsor Forward
Morton Betts Forward*
William Crake Forward
Thomas Hooman Forward
Robert Vidal Forward
Charles Wollaston Forward
Betts played under pseudonym AH Chequer

Royal Engineers (2-1-7)

Capt William Merriman Goalkeeper
Capt Francis Marindin (*Captain*) Full-Back
Lt George Addison Full-Back
Lt Alfred Goodwyn Half-Back
Lt Hugh Mitchell Forward
Lt Edmund Creswell Forward
Lt Henry Renny-Tailyour Forward
Lt Henry Rich Forward
Lt Herbert Muirhead Forward
Lt Edmond Cotter Forward
Lt Adam Bogle Forward

Umpires: **JH Giffard** (Royal Engineers)
      K Kirkpatrick (Wanderers)
Referee: **Alfred Stair** (Upton Park)

FRANCIS MARINDIN

A prominent player, administrator and official, Francis Arthur Marindin was one of the key figures in the development of association football. Marindin served in the Crimean War as a teenager, and had attained the rank of Captain in the 'Sappers' Corps by the time the Royal Engineers football club was formed in the 1860s. Known to his Army pals as Arthur, Marindin was an Old Etonian who was widely involved in the organisation of the Corps' many sporting activities. In 1869, he took over the captaincy of the football club from colleague William Merriman. Marindin's training drills were instrumental in the club becoming one of the best in the country, and he is credited as one of the leading proponents of the 'combination game'. Marindin was on the losing side in the 1872 and 1874 FA Cup finals, and missed Royal Engineers' victorious 1875 final as he was on duty overseas. By now a Major, Marindin also became heavily involved with football administration. An influential committee member, he served as president of the FA from 1874 until 1879. After relinquishing that post, and having retired from the Army, Major Marindin became Victorian football's most prominent referee. He took charge of eight FA Cup finals between 1880 and 1890, and developed a formidable no-nonsense reputation. Referred to by players as 'the *Majaw*', with the nickname delivered in an exaggerated posh accent, he was known to lecture teams on fair play before matches. He frowned upon professionalism, and didn't like the influx of Scottish players into the English game. After the 1888 final he was accused – probably unjustly – of favouring the all-English West Brom team over the more cosmopolitan Preston. After Preston lost, England captain Tinsley Lindley famously said, 'You cannot expect to win when playing against 11 men and the devil.' A remarkable character, Marindin also worked as the country's senior railway inspector, and led the committee that oversaw the introduction of electric lighting to London. He was knighted in 1897, and died in 1900, aged 61.

ORIGINAL FA CUP

The original Football Association Challenge Cup trophy was first presented to the man who had commissioned it, Wanderers captain and FA secretary CW Alcock, at a presentation dinner held at the Pall Mall Restaurant four weeks after his team had defeated Royal Engineers in the first ever final. FA Cup rules initially stated that any club that won the tournament three times would be awarded the trophy outright. Wanderers chalked up their third FA Cup final win in 1876, but Alcock decided to change the rules and hand the trophy back to the FA. Known as the 'Little Tin Idol', it continued to be presented to winning clubs (including Oxford University, Royal Engineers, Old Etonians, Clapham Rovers, Old Carthusians, Blackburn Olympic, Blackburn Rovers, West Brom, Preston, Wolves, Notts County, and the Wednesday) until 1895, when, while in the custody of Aston Villa, it was stolen from a Birmingham shoe shop window and melted down to make counterfeit coins. Villa were ordered to pay £25 for a replacement cup, which was used from 1896 through to 1910.

Aston Villa with the original FA Cup, 1887

VICTORIAN FOOTBALL BOOKS

The Laws of the Game, pub. Fred Lillywhite, 1863
The Winter Game: Rules of Football, JC Thring, 1863
Beeton's Football, Frederick Wood, 1866
Routledge's Handbook of Football, George Routledge, 1867
The Football Annual, CW Alcock, from 1868
Football: Our Winter Game, CW Alcock, 1874
Football: Its History for Five Centuries, Montague Shearman
          and JE Vincent, 1885
Athletics and Football, Montague Shearman, 1887
Football: A Popular Handbook, GA Hutchison, 1887
The Association Game, CW Alcock, 1890
Scottish Football Reminiscences and Sketches, David Drummond
          Bone, 1890
Famous Association Footballers, CW Alcock and Rowland Hill,
          1895
A Sporting Pilgrimage, Caspar Whitney, 1895
Football, A Budd & CB Fry, 1897
The Rise of the Leaguers: A History of the Football League,
          Tityrus (JAH Catton), 1897
Association Football, John Goodall, 1898
Association Football, NL Jackson, 1899
*The Real Football: A Sketch of the Development of the Association
          Game*, Tityrus (JAH Catton), 1900

QUARRY FALL

A 'serious and shocking accident' occurred during a match at Crookes, in Sheffield, in 1876. Walter Lawton, a 19-year-old player for the Broomhall Football Club, suffered a tragic misfortune. 'When in pursuit of the ball he ran headlong into a quarry, falling a distance of 30 feet on his head,' reported *Bell's Life*. The open field was not protected by fences, the paper said, adding that Lawton had been unconscious when taken to the infirmary, and was 'not likely to survive'.

BENEVOLENT FOOTBALLERS

In January 1872, the players of Hallam football club provided a touching example of the kindness of strangers. On their way to play a match at Stoney Middleton in Derbyshire, they noticed a poor old woman breaking rocks at the side of the road. Returning from the match, they made enquiries to find the woman, passed a hat around, and collected the small but no doubt helpful sum of six shillings and sixpence for her. 'It is to be hoped such a good example will be followed,' commented the *Derby Mercury*. 'It is a disgrace that any human being should have to break stones on a road, but that an old woman should be compelled to earn a living in that way is a standing reproach to the parish wherein she resides.'

THE OTHER ALCOCK

While CW Alcock is widely hailed as one of the founding fathers of modern football, his elder brother John is often overlooked. However, John did much to advance the game. He co-founded the influential Forest FC, and, as club captain, attended the inaugural meeting of the Football Association. As an FA committee member he was instrumental in championing Cambridge-style rules and outlawing hacking. Having helped to set the FA on its merry way, John left the committee in 1866, allowing CW to take over. John stopped playing football, and wasn't involved in Wanderers' cup triumphs. Unfortunately, his involvement in football was soon obscured by the events of a colourful personal life. His first marriage, to Catherine, ended in divorce, with John claiming she had been a prostitute when he met her, and Catherine claiming he had thrown bricks at her and beat her with a poker. Justice favoured the husband. Catherine was sent to a lunatic asylum, while John was free to pursue his non-footballing interests – mainly young women. He remarried twice, latterly to an 18-year-old, and went on to become a Tory councillor.

FIRST INTERNATIONAL

There was no Scottish FA in 1872, and football in Scotland was effectively run by the country's most powerful club – Queen's Park. The English FA had failed to generate sufficient Scottish interest to make the 'Alcock Internationals' work, so Queen's Park agreed to assemble a side that would properly represent Scotland. Club secretary Archibald Rae appealed for players from around the country, and two practices matches were held. In the event, however, the Scottish XI, selected by captain Robert Gardner, consisted entirely of Queen's Park players (although three of them also played for other clubs). The England team contained players from nine different clubs. Unluckily, England selector CW Alcock obtained a serious football injury in the run-up to the game and was forced to replace himself as captain with Cuthbert Ottaway. The international was played on 30 November at the West of Scotland Cricket Ground in Partick, Glasgow. Special buses ran to the ground from the city centre, and up to 4,000 spectators crowded around the roped-off pitch, with the gate receipts for the day totalling £103. Scotland wore dark blue shirts with lion crests, white knickerbockers, and blue and white hooped socks, while England wore white shirts bearing the three lions crest, white knickerbockers, and blue caps. England, playing with an adventurous 1-2-7 formation, showed superior individual skill, but Scotland, playing 2-2-6, adopted combination play, and showed dazzling teamwork. In a pretty even match, England had more goalscoring chances, but Scotland went closest to winning the game when a shot from Robert Leckie hit the tape and was judged by the umpires to have gone over, despite the cheers of the home crowd. *Bell's Life* described the game as 'a splendid display of football in the really scientific sense of the word, and a most determined effort on the part of the representatives of the two nationalities to overcome each other'. At the final whistle there had been no goals, but both sides were nevertheless afforded 'three hearty cheers'. The first international football match had been a success.

Scotland 0-0 England
30 November 1872
West of Scotland Cricket Ground, Glasgow

Scotland (2-2-6)

Robert Gardner (Queen's Park, *Captain*) Goalkeeper*
William Ker (Queen's Park & Granville) Back
Joseph Taylor (Queen's Park) Back
James Thomson (Queen's Park) Half-Back
James Smith (Queen's Park & South Norwood) Half-Back
Robert Smith (Queen's Park & South Norwood) Forward*
Robert Leckie (Queen's Park) Forward
Alexander Rhind (Queen's Park) Forward
Billy MacKinnon (Queen's Park) Forward
Jerry Weir (Queen's Park) Forward
David Wotherspoon (Queen's Park) Forward
Gardner and Robert Smith changed positions at half-time.

England (1-1-8)

Robert Barker (Hertfordshire Rangers) Goalkeeper**
Ernest Greenhalgh (Notts County) Back
Reginald de Courtenay Welch (Harrow Chequers) Half-Back
Frederick Chappell (Oxford University) Forward
William Maynard (1st Surrey Rifles) Forward**
John Brockbank (Cambridge University) Forward
Charles Clegg (The Wednesday) Forward
Arnold Kirke-Smith (Oxford University) Forward
Cuthbert Ottaway (Oxford University, *Captain*) Forward
Charles Chenery (Crystal Palace) Forward
Charles Morice (Barnes) Forward
**Barker and Maynard changed positions at half-time.*

Umpires: **CW Alcock** (Wanderers)
        Henry Norris Smith (Queen's Park)
Referee: **Willy Keay** (Queen's Park)

GOALKEEPERS WERE DIFFERENT

Many of the most important Victorian footballers were goal-keepers, including innovative Scottish international Robert Gardner, Ghanaian pioneer Arthur Wharton, and great exhibitionist William 'Fatty' Foulke. But in the earliest days of football the goalkeeping position didn't really exist. The original FA rules from 1863 allowed any player to take a 'fair catch' and set the ball down for a free-kick. The first mention of a goalkeeper came in the separate Sheffield rules, which stated: 'The goalkeeper is that player in the defending side who is for the time being nearest his own goal.' It was a 'last man back' rule, meaning teams could effectively play 'rush goalie'. In 1871 the FA updated its rules to outlaw handling of the ball except by a designated goalkeeper. 'A player shall not throw the ball nor pass it to another except in the case of the goalkeeper, who shall be allowed to use his hands for the protection of his goal,' the rules stated. But the Victorian goalkeeper was still very different to today's goalie. He was allowed to handle the ball anywhere within his own half of the field (that rule wasn't changed until 1912), and it was perfectly legal for burly forwards to knock the keeper over the goal-line with the ball. Victorian keepers wore the same kit and colours as their teammates, and only started wearing gloves towards the end of the 19th century. Darlington keeper and secretary Charles Samuel Craven wrote in 1886 about the attributes and techniques required: 'A good goal-keeper should not be less than 5ft 6in in height (the same in girth if he likes), active, cool, and have a good and quick eye. He should be a safe kick. In clearing the ball he should strike up in the air, so that the ball does not meet an opponent and rebound, He sometimes has eight yards to cover in next to no time, and as it is quicker to fall than to run, he should practice throwing himself down. When this art is acquired (and it cannot be done without practice) he will find it fairly useful.' One critic remarked, 'The only particular in which Craven coincides with what a good goalkeeper should be is in height.'

ROBERT GARDNER

Originally an outfield player, Scotland captain Robert Gardner started in goal for the first international match in 1872. He swapped positions with forward Robert Smith halfway through the game, but must have enjoyed his experience. Returning to his club Queen's Park – of which he was co-founder and captain – he kept goal on a regular basis, and soon became football's first great goalkeeper. Scottish football writer David Drummond Bone called him 'the most extraordinary player of his day'. 'When I remember the brilliant men who have since stood between the posts,' wrote Bone, 'I must confess that none ever used their hands and weight to greater advantage than Gardner.' His great innovation was narrowing the angle. Previously, goalkeepers would stick rigidly to the goal-line, but Gardner realised that advancing towards the ball made things more difficult for attacking players. Gardner died of tuberculosis in 1887, aged 39.

Scottish goalkeeper, likely Robert Gardner, the Graphic, 1872

GOLDEN TICKETS

Ahead of the much-anticipated first Scotland versus England international match, a correspondent going by the name of 'Fair Field and No Favour' wrote to the *Glasgow Herald* urging the match organisers to only admit spectators to the ground by ticket rather than cash on the gate. 'A good and fair game is of more consequence than large receipts,' he wrote, 'and it is impossible that the former can be properly under control if the admission of onlookers is not.' A previous match, he said, was 'nearly spoiled by the boasted 5,000 spectators'. However, 'Not Greedy' disagreed. 'Your correspondent wants the "favour" and "field" for himself, he having doubtless secured his ticket,' he responded. 'I do not know the committee of management, nor anyone who has tickets to dispose of, and it would be too bad if I had my journey to Partick for nothing. I have no doubt the committee will turn a deaf ear to your correspondent's unreasonable suggestion.'

EASIEST OF VICTORIES

The *Daily News* may have found 'very little interest' in an 1874 FA Cup first round tie between Wanderers and the 'comparatively unknown to fame' Farningham, but the remarkable scoreline was very interesting indeed. Wanderers won the toss, and pretty much everything else. 'The game was carried on nearly the whole of the time in the Farningham territory,' reported the newspaper, 'and, despite the excellent goalkeeping of WDO Greig, no less than 16 goals were kicked.' For the record, Robert Kingsford scored five, Charles Wollaston scored four, Charles Chenery, Hubert Heron and CW Alcock got two each, and Jarvis Kenrick scored the other goal in the 16-0 win. 'The match thus ended in the easiest of victories for the Wanderers.' Farningham keeper William Dallas Ochterlony Greig must have impressed, though. He switched clubs and won the FA Cup with Wanderers in the following season.

FRANCE FIRST

Which was the first French football club? A solid claim is held by Le Havre, founded by British expatriates as Le Havre Athletique in 1872. The club originally played a form of football that was closer to rugby, but by the mid-1890s it had adopted the association game. In 1899, the club became French champions by default after receiving byes in both the semi-final and the final. In the following year, Le Havre defeated famous Parisien champions Club Francais in the final to earn the championship by right. However, another side, FC Mulhouse, also hold a claim to being the first French football club. Although not founded until 1893 – by a pair of British students – Mulhouse didn't flirt with rugby, and instead played association football from the beginning. However, Mulhouse's claim is somewhat muddied by the fact that it is based in the Alsace-Lorraine region, which was in Germany, not France, at the time the club was formed. The club's original name was the more Germanic Fussball Club Mülhaussen. It became French after the First World War, reverted back to German during the Second World War, and is now back in the French league system. Does Le Havre or Mulhouse have the strongest claim to be France's first football club? Je ne sais pas.

ASSAULT WITH CHICKEN

Alexander Bonsor was one of football's first philanderers. Eton old boy Bonsor played for England in 1873 and 1875, scoring a goal in his first match and keeping goal in his second. He also played in four FA Cup finals, winning the competition in 1872 and 1873 with Wanderers. Away from football, however, he had a reputation as a womaniser, with a history of affairs and failed marriages. In 1895, his second wife Jeanne Marie filed for divorce, stating that Bonsor was a drunken adulterer who had on several occasions assaulted her – on one occasion with a chicken.

SCOTTISH FOOTBALL ASSOCIATION

Queen's Park had been acting as a de facto Scottish Football Association for several years, and the Glasgow club was the instigator of the meeting at which the proper SFA was formed in 1873. Eight clubs agreed to become founding members, at the meeting at Dewar's Hotel in Glasgow on 13 March, and resolved to 'form themselves into an association for the promotion of football according to the rules of the Football Association'. Archibald Campbell of Clydesdale was appointed SFA president, and Archibald Rae of Queen's Park was made secretary. The clubs also agreed to organise a challenge cup competition, and agreed to pay subscriptions to fund a trophy. Six of the eight founding members were based in Glasgow, with Kilmarnock and Vale of Leven the only clubs to join from outside of the city. Within a few weeks the SFA's membership had doubled, and 18 teams competed in the first Scottish Cup competition in the 1873-74 season. The cup was won, of course, by the then-invincible Queen's Park.

SFA FOUNDING MEMBERS, 1873

Clydesdale (Glasgow)
Dumbreck (Glasgow)
Eastern (Glasgow)
Granville (Glasgow)
Kilmarnock
Queen's Park (Glasgow)
Third Lanark (Glasgow)
Vale of Leven

Additional members for season 1873-74:
Alexandra Athletic (Glasgow), Blythswood (Glasgow), Callander, Dumbarton, Rovers (Glasgow), Renton, Southern (Glasgow), Western (Glasgow)

ENGLAND VS SCOTLAND INTERNATIONALS

5 Mar 1870	England	1–1	Scotland	AI
19 Nov 1870	England	1-0	Scotland	AI
25 Feb 1871	England	1–1	Scotland	AI
17 Nov 1871	England	2-1	Scotland	AI
24 Feb 1872	England	1-0	Scotland	AI
30 Nov 1872	Scotland	0–0	England	FR
8 Mar 1873	England	4-2	Scotland	FR
7 Mar 1874	Scotland	2-1	England	FR
6 Mar 1875	England	2-2	Scotland	FR
4 Mar 1876	Scotland	3–0	England	FR
3 Mar 1877	England	1-3	Scotland	FR
2 Mar 1878	Scotland	7–2	England	FR
5 Apr 1879	England	5-4	Scotland	FR
13 Mar 1880	Scotland	5-4	England	FR
12 Mar 1881	England	1-6	Scotland	FR
11 Mar 1882	Scotland	5–1	England	FR
10 Mar 1883	England	2-3	Scotland	FR
15 Mar 1884	Scotland	1-0	England	BH
21 Mar 1885	England	1–1	Scotland	BH
27 Mar 1886	Scotland	1–1	England	BH
19 Mar 1887	England	2-3	Scotland	BH
17 Mar 1888	Scotland	0–5	England	BH
13 Apr 1889	England	2-3	Scotland	BH
5 Apr 1890	Scotland	1–1	England	BH
4 Apr 1891	England	2-1	Scotland	BH
2 Apr 1892	Scotland	1-4	England	BH
1 Apr 1893	England	5-2	Scotland	BH
7 Apr 1894	Scotland	2–2	England	BH
6 Apr 1895	England	3-0	Scotland	BH
4 Apr 1896	Scotland	2–1	England	BH
3 Apr 1897	England	1-2	Scotland	BH
2 Apr 1898	Scotland	1–3	England	BH
8 Apr 1899	England	2-1	Scotland	BH
7 April 1900	Scotland	4–1	England	BH

AI: 'Unofficial' Alcock International
FR: Friendly International
BH: British Home Championship

FUSSBALL

The first German football club was Dresden FC, formed in 1874 by Englishmen working in the city. Sometimes referred to as Dresden English FC, the club had around 70 members who would meet at the Güntzwiesen park to train and play matches. Contemporary reports described young men playing in coloured kits comprising woollen or silk jerseys, knicker-bockers, stockings, and 'very comfortable shoes or boots'. The club is associated with the present day Dresdner SC, which was formed in 1898 by German members of the Dresden English club. Football's profile was briefly raised when the Oxford University team toured Germany in 1875. However, it would be more than 10 years before the game really caught on. Matches were played in Berlin and Hamburg between British expats, but football remained a curiosity to the locals, and no football pitches existed. Germany's oldest surviving football club is BFC Germania 1888, which was formed in that year by three Berlin brothers and their schoolmates. The club played on the Tempelhofer field, which would later become the site of Tempelhof Airport. (Since the airport closed in 2008, Tempelhof has once more become a venue at which football is played.) Germania was a founding member of the country's first football league, the BDF (Association of German Footballers), which was running from 1890 until 1892. Germania won the league in its first season, thus becoming Germany's first football champions. Another of the oldest German football clubs is SV Hamburg. Formed in 1887, it began playing football in 1891, due to the influence of several British members. TSV 1814 Friedland was, as its name accurately reflects, formed in 1814. However, the gymnastics and sports club didn't start playing football until the 1950s. TSV 1860 Munich was, rather confusingly, formed in 1848, but didn't play football until 1899. The DFB (German Football Association) was founded in 1900. Fussball-Club Bayern München, or FC Bayern Munich, also formed in 1900.

BILLY MOSFORTH

England winger Billy Mosforth, 'the Sheffield Dodger', was known for his small stature, his devastating speed, and his ability to bend a football – pioneering what was then known as the 'screw shot'. Journalist Jimmy Catton called Mosforth a 'great artist', and his ability to dribble the ball the entire length of the pitch made him an early fans' favourite. He began his career at Sheffield Albion, but switched between various Sheffield teams, including Wednesday and United. On one occasion he was said to have switched sides from Hallam FC to the Wednesday just before kick-off after a spectator offered him '10 bob and free drinks' if he changed his shirt. He played nine times for England, scoring three goals. In April 1879, Mosforth played against Scotland at the Oval. At half-time England were 4-1 down, but by full-time they had won 5-4, and Mosforth was mobbed by jubilant spectators. Even the Scottish umpire, Arthur Kinnaird, rushed over to congratulate Mosforth, and to ask where he got his marvellous speed from. 'They carried me off the field afterwards,' said Mosforth, 'so I must have played pretty well.'

CAMBRIAN FOOTBALL

In January 1876, a proposal was published in the *Field* for an international football match between Scotland and Wales. The proposal caught the eye of Samuel Llewelyn Kenrick, a solicitor from Ruabon, near Wrexham. Kenrick had played football in England for Shropshire Wanderers, reaching the FA Cup semi-finals in 1875. Back in Wales, he helped form the Ruabon-based Druids club, and played for them in a series of friendlies, including matches against English and Scottish clubs. Kenrick responded in the *Field*, stating that he would arrange test matches and raise a 'Cambrian XI' to take on Scotland. He duly set up the Cambrian Football Association to facilitate the arrangements, and selected a team that featured six Druids players – including himself. Only one of the Welsh team was from South Wales, leading to allegations of Northern bias. The match was played at the West of Scotland Cricket Ground. Kenrick captained his country, playing at full-back. Of the Welsh players, reports said he 'showed decidedly best'. Wales were comfortably beaten 4-0, but from an organisational point of view the match was a success. A meeting was held at Kenrick's local pub, the Wynnstay Arms Hotel in Ruabon, during which the Cambrian Football Association was renamed the Football Association of Wales. Kenrick was appointed chairman and secretary. In 1877, he instigated the Welsh Cup – which he won in 1881 as captain of Druids. Described as a 'small, muscular player', Kenrick made five appearances for Wales. The last one, in 1881, was highly unusual. Kenrick had retired from football, and attended the England versus Wales match in Blackburn as a spectator. But, after a Wales player missed his train, Kenrick was asked to take his place. The veteran played in 'long tweed trousers, ordinary boots and a smart Oxford shirt', but gave a 'splendid performance' – until his knee gave way, and he was forced to leave the field. Nevertheless, his efforts helped Wales beat England 1-0 – the nation's first international victory. Now regarded as the father of Welsh football, Kenrick died in 1933.

ASTON VILLA

The most successful football club of the Victorian era was formed in 1874 by four youngsters from the Aston Villa Wesleyan Chapel cricket team. One of those youngsters was Walter Price, who was named Aston Villa FC's first captain. Villa initially struggled to find opposition and purpose, but the club's fortunes quickly improved following the arrival of George Ramsay. The 21-year-old Scot impressed teammates with his football skills and knowledge of the game, and was appointed the new club captain. Ramsay understood that, in order to succeed, the club had to find an enclosed ground and generate gate money. He was instrumental in setting Villa up at its first permanent home – Perry Barr. Ramsay was succeeded as club captain by another Scot, Archie Hunter, and it was Hunter who led Villa to their first FA Cup final triumph, in 1887, when they defeated West Brom 2-0. Hunter and Dennis Hodgetts scored the goals. Villa president William McGregor created the Football League in 1888, and the club finished second in the league's inaugural season. Villa won the league in 1894, the FA Cup in 1895, the league again in 1896, and then the league and cup double in 1897. The double-winning team was captained by Albert Evans, marshalled in defence by Jimmy Crabtree, and spearheaded up front by John Campbell and Fred Wheldon. Both Campbell and Wheldon scored in the 1897 Cup final, and Wheldon top-scored for the club with 22 goals over the season. The club's manager during this incredibly successful period was the still-influential George Ramsay. Further league wins followed in 1897 and 1899, taking Villa's major honour tally during the Victorian era to eight – three FA Cups and five league titles. The club moved to Aston Lower Grounds in 1897, building a stadium that would eventually come to be called Villa Park. New stars such as Billy Garraty and Billy George emerged towards the end of the 19th century. The Edwardian era was pretty good to Villa, too, but the club's successes of the Victorian era will never be forgotten.

MOST SUCCESSFUL CLUBS

Aston Villa won eight major honours during the Victorian era – three FA Cups and five league titles. Blackburn Rovers and Wanderers each won five FA Cups, with the cup being considered much more prestigious than the league at the time. Only three clubs – Aston Villa, Preston North End and Sheffield United – won both the league and the cup in the Victorian era. Preston North End and Aston Villa both won 'the double' in a single season – in 1888-89 and 1896-97 respectively.

Team	FA Cup	League	Total
Aston Villa	3	5	8
Blackburn Rovers	5		5
Wanderers	5		5
Preston North End	1	2	3
Sunderland		3	3
Old Etonians	2		2
West Bromwich Albion	2		2
Sheffield United	1	1	2
Blackburn Olympic	1		1
Bury	1		1
Clapham Rovers	1		1
Nottingham Forest	1		1
Notts County	1		1
Old Carthusians	1		1
Oxford University	1		1
Royal Engineers	1		1
The Wednesday	1		1
Wolverhampton Wanderers	1		1
Everton		1	1

REDUCED INTERNATIONAL

The first international match between England and Wales was curious for several reasons, in part due to bad weather and a murder trial. The game was played at the Kennington Oval on 18 January 1879 'with snow lying several inches deep, while a cheerless mixture of snow and sleet was falling'. As an indication of how terrible the weather was, as few as 85 spectators turned up – representing the lowest ever attendance at an international match involving 'home nation' teams. England kicked off without William Clegg, a solicitor, who was busy representing the notorious murderer Charles Peace. Wales were effectively reduced to 10 men when centre-forward Dennis Heywood received an early injury, although he struggled on. Clegg arrived with 20 minutes gone, and entered the action with England already two goals up, through Tom Sorby and Herbert Whitfield. It was decided that 90 minutes of play was impossible, so half-time was called after just 30 minutes. The referee, by the way, was Segar Bastard. The second 30 minutes saw Wales improve, and score a goal through Henry Davies. But, when the truncated match ended, England had held on to win 2-1. (Charles Peace, meanwhile, despite Clegg's best efforts, was found guilty of murder and executed.)

WHITE STUFF

Inclement weather rarely prevented the Victorians from playing football, and many significant matches were played in layers of snow. Football was, after all, 'the winter game'. *Northern Echo* football columnist Off-Side joked, 'Football! The word sounds delightful with snow lying nearly a foot deep.' *The Graphic*, meanwhile, commented, 'Snow certainly has an advantage over mud, in that it does not disfigure the players so frightfully, and the game is pretty enough on the white ground, the snow kicked about by the players forming at times a kind of cloud about them.'

ARTHUR KINNAIRD

Arthur Kinnaird, born in 1847, was perhaps football's first celebrity – a kind of 19th century David Beckham – cutting a very recognisable dash on the field in his shaggy red beard and signature white cricket trousers. Kinnaird (or Arthur Fitzgerald Kinnaird, 11th Lord Kinnaird KT (Order of the Thistle), to give him his full title) was an English-born Scottish Laird, who was capped by Scotland courtesy of his Perthshire roots. At club level, he played in nine FA Cup finals, and won five of them – three with Wanderers and two with Old Etonians. After winning his fifth final, the noted exhibitionist celebrated by standing on his head in front of the Oval pavilion. Kinnaird played up front, at half-back, and in goal when the fancy took him. In the 1877 cup final, while keeping goal for Wanderers, he caught a seemingly innocuous shot and fell backwards, carrying the ball over the goal-line. It was the very first recorded own goal, confusing spectators and newspaper reporters alike. (Kinnaird's blushes were saved – Wanderers won the cup in extra time.) Regarded as an honest and gentlemanly player, he was nevertheless known to be a tough tackler. A story linked to Kinnaird has his wife expressing her fear that he may one day come home from a football match with a broken leg. A friend, thought to be CW Alcock, advised her not to worry: 'If he does come home with a broken leg, it will not be his own.' 'As a player, in any position, [Kinnaird] was an exemplar of manly robust football,' wrote Jimmy Catton. An all-round sportsman, Kinnaird was also a champion sprinter, swimmer, tennis player and canoeist. Away from sport, he was a noted philanthropist, a supporter of the 'ragged schools' for destitute children, and president of the YMCA and YWCA. In his working life, he was one of the first directors of Barclays Bank. He inherited his Lordship in 1887. Kinnaird was also an important football administrator. He had been an FA committee member since the age of 21, and was appointed president in 1890. He held the role until his death in 1923, aged 75.

Arthur Kinnaird, 1899

INSTANT REPLAYS

The 1877-78 FA Cup competition produced two epic encounters that took weeks to resolve. The first was a third round tie between Old Harrovians and Cambridge University. Initially played at the Oval on 2 February 1878, the match resulted in a 2-2 draw, and a replay was arranged for the following week. After 90 minutes, the score was again 2-2. It was mutually agreed to play 30 minutes of extra time, and then a further 15 minutes, before darkness put an end to proceedings with the sides unable to be separated. 'When Greek meets Greek,' commented *the Graphic*. A further replay was arranged for the following Saturday. The paper suggested that gas lamps might be used to allow the game to be played to a finish: 'Perhaps Mr Alcock, who does so much to keep up the spirit of football, will thoughtfully arrange a series of gas jets around the ground so that this dogged contest may be at an end before Sunday morning.' Finally, on 16 February, the third round tie was settled, with Old Harrovians winning 2-0. Meanwhile, on the same weekend, the fourth round was underway, and Oxford University were playing Royal Engineers. When the referee blew the final whistle, Engineers were leading 3-2, and the majority of the spectators - and newspaper reporters - went home in the belief that the tie was over. However, it quickly transpired that the referee had accidentally blown a quarter of an hour early. The teams came back out, played another 15 minutes, and Oxford scored an equaliser. Unbeknown to many, the match ended 3-3. In a replay, on 27 February, Oxford took a two goal lead, only for Engineers to fight back to 2-2. With the score level at full-time, 'after a lengthy discussion', it was agreed to play 30 minutes of extra time. But there were no more goals. Another replay followed, on 12 March. After an exciting match, the tie finally arrived at what *Bell's Life* called 'a solution of the knotty point', with Engineers winning 4-2. Engineers went on to beat Old Harrovians in the semi-final but, no doubt exhausted, they lost in the final to Wanderers.

RANGERS

The oldest of Glasgow's Old Firm clubs, Rangers was formed in 1872 by four teenagers – Peter Campbell, William McBeath, and brothers Peter and Moses McNeil. The club played its first match at Flesher's Haugh on Glasgow Green in May 1872, drawing 0-0 with Callendar. Another McNeil, Harry, guested for Rangers, alongside his Queen's Park (and later Scotland) teammate Billy MacKinnon. The founding members subsequently recruited 16-year-old pal Tom Vallance, who became the club's first captain. A second match, against the original Clyde club, saw Rangers win 11-0, in new blue jerseys. Three of the club's founders died in unhappy circumstances. Peter Campbell was killed in 1883 when the coal steamer he worked on sank in a storm in the Bay of Biscay. Peter McNeil died in a Glasgow insane asylum in 1901. And William McBeath died in a poorhouse in 1917 and was buried in a pauper's grave.

CELTIC

Celtic was founded by Marist Catholic priest Andrew Kerins, known as Brother Walfrid, who was originally from County Sligo in Ireland. Walfrid worked as a teacher in Glasgow, and the football club was formed with the intention of raising money for poor children in the east end of the city. The club's first meeting was held at St Mary's church hall on Forbes Street in November 1887. Walfrid suggested the name Celtic to reflect combined Scottish and Irish roots, using the correct Victorian pronunciation of *Seltik*. The club's first match was played at the old Celtic Park in front of 2,000 spectators on 29 May 1888 – and it was also the first Old Firm match. The Celtic team comprised players from several other clubs with Irish connections, while Rangers fielded a mostly reserve side. First spoils went to Celtic – with the newcomers winning 5-2. The *Scottish Umpire* magazine commented: 'It would appear as if the newly-formed club has a bright future before it.'

FLOODLIGHT FAILURE

In 1878, the year that Joseph Swan patented the incandescent light bulb, the first floodlit game of football took place – but it wasn't a particular success. The match was played on an October night at Bramall Lane between two Sheffield Football Association sides. 30,000 spectators turned up to witness the curious experiment, arranged in part to promote the local Tasker electrical company. 'The match was announced to commence at half-past seven o'clock, and considerably before that hour the roads to Bramall Lane were completely besieged,' observed the *Sheffield and Rotherham Independent*. 'The wonder was where all the people came from.' The *Manchester Times* explained how the match was illuminated: 'The electric light was thrown on the grounds from four lamps, 30 feet from the ground. Behind each goal was placed a portable engine, each of which drove two dynamo machines, one for each light. The illuminating power was equal to 8,000 standard candles.' Unfortunately, the lights didn't cover the whole pitch, and couldn't be moved fast enough to keep up with play. The *Manchester Times* reported other problems, too: 'Some amusement was caused by the brilliance of the light, which dazzled the players, and caused some strange blunders.' 'A serious accident, by which four persons were more or less injured, occurred during the display,' reported the *Sheffield and Rotherham Independent*. 'A young man drove through the crowd with a pair of horses attached to a waggonette. He did not stop, it is alleged, to let the people get out of the way, and the consequence was four persons were knocked down and injured.' One man, the paper reported, 'was trampled upon by one of the horses and was severely cut about the head.' For the record, the Blues, captained by William Clegg, beat the Reds 2-0. Although an interesting spectacle, the experiment was an expensive failure. Subsequent illuminated matches at the Oval in London and elsewhere also failed to impress, and floodlights weren't properly introduced to football for another 70 years.

Match played by electric light at the Oval, Illustrated News, 1878

TEMERITY OF BUMBLEDOM

In 1880, Justice of the Peace John Cooksey called for all forms of football to be banned following the tragic death of 19-year-old clerk Stanley Gibbs during a rugby match in Southampton. Gibbs slipped during a scrimmage and was trampled. 'He felt something snap, and lost all sense of feeling in the lower part of his body,' reported the *Graphic*. He died a few days later, having broken his spine. The coroner recorded a verdict of accidental death, but recommended that the rules of rugby be changed to prevent further accidents. The JP's call to ban all forms of football was met by opposition from the *Athletic News*, which called Cooksey 'maternally disposed', and said he wore a look of the 'senile temerity of bumbledom'. The ban wasn't enforced, but the tragic incident lessened the town's enthusiasm for rugby, and persuaded a group of teachers to organise Southampton's first association match. Five years later, in 1885, St Mary's Young Men's Association formed an association football club – later renamed Southampton FC.

FALSE ZULU DAWN

The Zulu War, fought in South Africa in 1879 (and immortalised in movies *Zulu* and *Zulu Dawn*), cost more than 1,700 British and 6,000 Zulu lives. However, within a few months of the Battles of Isandlwana and Rorke's Drift, a Zulu football team was touring Britain, playing exhibition matches in front of thousands of delighted spectators. Led by Cetawayo, the Zulu King who had defeated the British at Isandlwana, and his brother Dabulamanzi, the hero of Rorke's Drift, the team played a warm-up match in Scarborough, and then travelled to take on a Sheffield FA XI in an exhibition aimed at raising funds for the families of (British) soldiers killed in the conflict. Around 2,000 spectators crammed into Bramall Lane to watch the spectacle. However, all was not as it might at first have appeared. 'It may be necessary to state that the Zulus were only Zulus in name,' reported the *Sheffield and Rotherham Independent*. 'They were not black men, but veritable whites.' The 'Zulus' were actually local footballers who had blacked-up their faces with burnt cork, and covered their bodies with black jerseys and stockings. They wore feathers on their heads and white beads around their necks, and they carried spears and shields that, it was claimed, 'were actually brought from the battlefields of Zululand'. 'Cetawayo' was in fact T Buttery of Sheffield Exchange FC, and 'Dabulamanzi' was actually England international Jack Hunter, who would go on to win the FA Cup with Blackburn Olympic. 'The Zulus proved quite as good, and even better than their masters, for they succeeded in defeating them by five goals to four,' said the *Independent*. 'The play at times created a considerable amount of amusement, and the spectators appeared to enjoy the proceedings immensely.' However, as the Zulu team's tour moved on, to Chesterfield, Nottingham and Edinburgh, it transpired that the players were being paid for their services – at a time when professionalism was still outlawed. The players concerned were banned by the Sheffield FA, and the Zulus team was disbanded, never to black up again.

SCOTCH CANADIANS

In 1880, the Scottish FA decided to organise a tour of Canada and the United States. The tour had been encouraged by the Governor General of Canada, and support was offered by the Carlton Club of Toronto, which is thought to have been Canada's first football club, and participated in the first association game played in Canada, in Toronto in 1876. A squad of 24 players 'volunteered for service in the New World'. The great Tom Vallance of Rangers was appointed captain, and William Somers of Queen's Park was vice-captain. Other notable squad members included Robert Gardner, Harry McNeil and George Ker. Young SFA secretary William Dick headed to Canada to make arrangements. In order to raise funds for the tour, a series of exhibition matches was played, with the tour squad, dubbed the 'Scotch Canadians', playing in Glasgow, Newcastle, Blackburn and Nottingham, to huge public interest. John Goldie of the Carlton club travelled over from Canada to participate in the tour, acting as umpire for the Scotch Canadians. The tour team looked formidable (they defeated Rangers 1-0, beat a Newcastle team 5-0, thrashed Blackburn Rovers 8-1, and beat Nottingham Forest 2-0), and large crowds of several thousand at each game must surely have generated sufficient funds. However, in April 1880, the SFA was rocked by the sudden death of tour organiser Dick. He'd returned from Canada, and died at home in Glasgow. He was just 29, although he'd worked for the SFA for more than 10 years. In his short life he'd captained Third Lanark, founded the *Scottish Football Annual*, and refereed a couple of Scottish internationals. A benefit match was played between Queen's Park and Clapham Rovers – the Scottish and English cup holders – and the SFA had an impressive memorial, featuring a carved thistle and a football, installed at the Glasgow Necropolis in tribute to Dick's 'private worth and faithful services'. The tour was scrapped, and it would be almost 10 years before a British national side eventually ventured overseas.

SCOTCHED RUMOUR

Tom Vallance was one of the founding members of Rangers Football Club, and is one of the most important figures in its history. The club's first captain, Vallance was an imposing full-back who made seven international appearances for Scotland. He was a one-club man, who devoted much of his life to Rangers. However, in 1880 the *Blackburn Standard* reported that Vallance, 'the best back in the world', had been approached by prominent Lancashire club Darwen to play for them in England. The report came to the attention of Vallance, and a letter from the Rangers captain appeared in the *Standard* in the following week. 'I cannot understand from whence you received your information,' wrote Vallance, 'as at no time have I ever been requested to play for Darwen. The friendly feelings which I have always entertained towards the Darwen Club, coupled with the vivid recollections of the warm-hearted and handsome manner in which I was treated when playing against them last season prompts me to make this reply, which I trust you will find space for insertion.' After illness curtailed his playing career, 'Honest Tom' was appointed club president, and did much to establish Rangers as one of the biggest clubs in Britain.

GLASGOW VS SHEFFIELD

A reminder that London was not the centre of the football world was provided on an annual basis by the high profile matches between the football associations of Glasgow and Sheffield, which began in 1874. The first encounter, played at Bramall Lane under Sheffield Rules in front of 5,000 spectators, ended in a 2-2 draw. Nine members of the Glasgow side were Scottish internationals, and the team wore Scotland jerseys. Glasgow dominated subsequent games, winning nine out of the next 10. The fixture continued annually until 1938, and was played on an occasional basis through to 1960.

BLACKBURN ROVERS

One of the great FA Cup teams of the Victorian era, Blackburn Rovers was founded in 1875 by public school old boys John Lewis and Arthur Constantine. The pair organised a meeting at the Leger Hotel on 5 November 1875, at which 17 men agreed to join the club. Little football was played in Blackburn at the time, and the new club got off to a slow start. Rovers played their early games at Oozehead, a boggy piece of farm-land with a pond in the middle that had to be covered over with planks of wood before games could be played. In 1878, Rovers became inaugural members of the Lancashire Football Association. The club had two key local rivals – Darwen, which adopted association rules in 1875, and Blackburn Olympic, which was formed in 1878. Both of those rivals enjoyed early success – with Olympic winning the FA Cup in 1883. At that point it looked likely that struggling Rovers could fold. However, in the following season the club went on a remarkable FA Cup run, beating the likes of Upton Park and Notts County on the way to the final at the Oval. There they defeated Queen's Park 2-1, with goals from Jimmys Douglas and Forrest. Rovers met Queen's Park in the FA Cup final again in 1885, and Forrest scored again, alongside James Brown, in a 2-0 win. In 1886, Rovers defeated West Brom 2-0 after a replay to claim a third consecutive FA Cup win. James Brown and Joe Sowerbutts scored the goals. Scotsman Thomas Mitchell, who managed Rovers for 12 years, was instrumental during the club's glory years. After becoming inaugural members of the Football League in 1888, Rovers returned to the Oval as FA Cup finalists in 1890, and thrashed The Wednesday 6-1, with William Townley scoring a hat-trick. Nat Walton, Jack Southworth and Joe Lofthouse also scored. And Rovers did it again in 1891, beating Notts County 3-1 in their fifth FA Cup win. Townley, Southworth and Geordie Dewar got the goals. By this time, Rovers had a new home – Ewood Park. There were no further cup wins in the Victorian era, but Rovers had left an indelible mark on football history.

SHINPADS

The invention of the shinpad, or 'shin guard', is credited to Sam Weller Widdowson, the Nottingham Forest captain, who, legend says, first cut down a pair of cricket pads to protect his shins around 1874. Widdowson (named by his father after the character Sam Weller from Charles Dickens' *The Pickwick Papers*) fastened his customised pads to the outside of his football stockings with leather straps. The idea didn't immediately take off. In fact, Widdowson faced some derision for having the gall to protect the most vulnerable parts of his legs. However, by 1880 shin guards were being hailed as 'the great desideratum for all football players'. That was down to the marketing efforts of the great cricketer and Notts County co-founder Richard Daft, who owned a sports equipment shop at Lister Gate, Nottingham. Daft placed advertisements in the national press for his catalogue service, via which he also provided footballs, inflators, jerseys, goalposts and flags. The shin guard was incorporated into the FA's Laws of the Game in 1881. By that time Widdowson, now an England international, had registered his invention, and was selling his own range of 'new improved shin guards' via Daft's catalogues. In 1890, a Mr JB Haslam of Bolton patented the 'pneumatic shin guard'. Unfortunately for Mr Haslam, that daft idea never made it into the Daft catalogue.

DYNAMITE FOOTBALL

'What next in football?' asked *Bell's Life* in March 1882. 'We notice that a match has been played and won by a club called "Dynamite". The explanation of the name consists of the fact that the Dynamite club is composed of young men employed by the Ardeer Dynamite Company, who have a large establishment at that small Ayrshire town.' The British Dynamite Factory in Ardeer was the largest explosives manufacturing plant in the world, and employed almost 13,000 people.

Sam Weller Widdowson, 1881

WIDDOWSON'S PEAK

In 1879-80, Nottingham Forest thrashed Notts County and Blackburn Rovers on the way to the fourth round of the FA Cup. There, Forest met Sheffield FC, who proved to be a tough opponent. Indeed, Sheffield led 2-1 with just two minutes left to play. Then Forest's Sam Widdowson set off on a mazy dribble, beating the Sheffield defence, and firing a brilliant equaliser past keeper Michael Ellison. The Sheffield players were furious, and, at the end of the 90 minutes, they refused to play extra time. Sheffield stormed off, but Forest stayed on the pitch. Widdowson waited five minutes, then, when it was clear the opposition wouldn't be returning, he booted the ball between Sheffield's empty goal-posts. 3-2 to Forest. Sheffield's appeal was rejected, and Forest ended up reaching the FA Cup semi-finals, where they lost to Oxford University.

A WANT OF ENERGY

The 1880 FA Cup final, contested at the Oval by Clapham Rovers and Oxford University, is notable for the colourful names that appeared on the team sheet, which, even by Victorian standards, could be considered exotic. The only goal of the game came with just 10 minutes left to play. A left-wing cross from Clapham's Francis Sparks was missed by Oxford back Charles James Stuart King, and finished past keeper Percival Chase Parr by Clopton Lloyd-Jones. A *Bell's Life* correspondent subsequently offered his reasoning for Oxford's defeat: 'Would it not be advisable that football players should keep all their energy for the match,' wrote 'A Spectator', 'in place of throwing away a great deal of it before the game commences by astonishing the multitude at the splendid kicks they can give the ball? At the Oval on Saturday two or three of the Oxford players indulged at this for a quarter of an hour at least before the match began. As I thought some of them showed a want of energy towards the end of the game, may this not have had something to do with their losing it?'

1880 FA CUP FINAL TEAM SHEET

Clapham Rovers:
Reginald Halsey Birkett
Robert Andrew Muter
  Macindoe Ogilvie
Edgar Field
Vincent Weston
Norman Coles Bailey
Arthur J Stanley
Harold Brougham
Francis Sparks
Felix Barry
Edward Ram
Clopton Allen Lloyd-Jones

Oxford University:
Percival Chase Parr
Claude William Wilson

Charles James Stuart King
Francis Phillips
Bertram Rogers
Reginald Heygate
Rev George Borlise Childs
John Eyre
Francis Crowdy
Evelyn Harry Hill
John Birbeck Lubbock

FOOTBALL CONFERENCE

In April 1880, a conference of football associations was held at the Great Western Hotel in Birmingham. Present were CW Alcock of the Football Association, Mr Hamilton of the Scottish Football Association, Mr Manners of the Football Association of Wales, William Pierce Dix of the Sheffield Association, plus representatives from the Edinburgh, Birmingham, Cheshire, Lancashire, Berks and Bucks, Staffordshire, and Ayrshire FAs. There were two key issues to be debated. The first was the throw-in. The 'London throw-in' rule used and favoured by the Football Association allowed a throw at any angle from the touch-line. However, the 'Scottish throw-in', which had also been used in Sheffield, had to be thrown at a right angle from the touch-line, similar to that for a rugby union line-out. The majority of delegates favoured the 'London throw-in', and it was recommended that be adopted by all associations. The second key issue was the division of the country for the arrangement of North versus South representative matches. It was decided that the line of division should be drawn at the southern edge of Birmingham, and that all points beyond should be classed as 'the North'. The first North versus South match was played on 3 March 1880 at the Oval, with Jack Hunter of Sheffield Heeley and Charles Wollaston of Wanderers (both England internationals) the respective captains. It ended as a goalless draw. Subsequent contests tended to be won by the 'home' team, with the South winning in London, and the North victorious in Sheffield and Derby. At a second conference of football associations, held at the Albion Hotel in Manchester, a unanimous recommendation was made to change the name of the Football Association to the 'National Football Association'. That recommendation was rejected, but the conferences were successful in helping to assimilate universal rules across the country. The meeting of associations also set a precedent for the foundation of the International Football Association Board, which was formed by the English, Scottish, Welsh and Irish FAs in 1886.

WEST BROMWICH ALBION

Formed in 1878 as West Bromwich Strollers, West Brom was
originally a works team for the Salter spring scales factory.
The name 'Strollers' came from the fact that the players
regularly strolled two miles to the nearby town of Wednes-
bury to buy their footballs. The club played its first match, a
goalless draw with workers from the nearby Hudson soap
factory, on 23 November 1878. By 1880, the club had changed
its name to West Bromwich Albion, with the 'Albion' suffix
referring to a district of the town rather than the archaic
name for Britain. The club competed in the Birmingham
Senior Cup, and won the Staffordshire Cup, while establishing
homes first at the Four Acres ground, and then at Stoney
Lane. After West Brom turned professional in 1885, the first
team were compensated in line with the club's increasing
gates. The second team, however, received no pay rise, and
duly went on strike. The end result was that the entire second
team resigned, and had to be replaced. It was around this
time that the club began to make its mark on the FA Cup.
West Brom reached the final in 1886 and 1887, and then won
the cup in 1888, beating the mighty Preston North End. West
Brom were regarded as underdogs against the ultra-confident
Preston, whose players had requested to be photographed
with the trophy before kick-off. But West Brom captain Jem
Bayliss led his side to victory, scoring one of the goals in a 2-1
win. Bayliss, from Tipton, went on to play for England. All of
West Brom's cup-winning players were local men, with no
Preston-style Scottish imports. The cup-winning goalkeeper
was 6ft 4in and 13 stone Bob Roberts, who had been a versa-
tile outfield player until his large frame was placed between
the goalposts. West Brom become founder members of the
Football League when it formed in 1888. In 1892, the club
comfortably beat rivals Aston Villa 3-0 to win the FA Cup for a
second time. Jasper Geddes, Sammy Nicholls and Jack Rey-
nolds scored the goals. West Brom met Villa in the final again
in 1895, but this time lost 1-0.

FATHER OF MODERN FOOTBALL

Unlike some of his contemporaries, CW Alcock's contribution to the development of the game was recognised at the time. In 1875, while still in the twilight of his career as a player, he was celebrated as the 'father of modern football' by the *Graphic*. That designation was reused when he retired from playing in 1876 (although the *Graphic*, in an example of toilet humour, managed to call him 'WC Alcock'). 'He retires with his honours thick upon him,' the paper noted, 'and his name will long be known as the father of modern football.' In 1881, Alcock was presented with a testimonial, paid for by subscriptions of players from around the country, in recognition of his service to the game. At a ceremony at the Freemasons' Tavern, where the Football Association had been formed 18 years earlier, Francis Marindin presented Alcock with a silver inkstand, a pair of silver candlesticks, and a cheque for £330. Marindin also presented the following resolution: 'That the committee, in their name and in the name of all the players scattered throughout the kingdom, tender to Mr Alcock the expression of their sincere thanks for the zeal with which he has discharged his duties, and further record their unanimous conviction that the success which has attended the Association in all its undertakings and the established position the game now occupies among the winter sports, are due in no ordinary degree to the loyal and untiring devotion with which he has ever sought to promote its interests and prosperity.' Marindin added that in 1863 the game had been 'almost entirely unknown', but now almost every town and village in the country had a football club. That, Marindin said, was due 'chiefly to Mr Alcock's untiring zeal and energy'. In response, Alcock said he was 'highly proud' that football players had come together to show their appreciation to him, but he took time to highlight the contributions made by others. He said he preferred to think that the testimonial had come about through 'a desire on the part of Associationists to commemorate the wonderful progress of their game'.

'So it has come at last!' cried *Bell's Life*. 'What next?' The event that had the paper so agitated was a women's football match, played in May 1881 at Easter Road, Edinburgh. 'Several years ago there was a rage for silly displays of certain kinds of athletics by women, but we thought the time had passed,' said *Bell's*. 'To give the arrangement the semblance of an international event the girls had the cheek to designate the farce England v Scotland.' The 22 women, who had practised in a Glasgow hall ahead of the match, were all aged between 18 and 24. Scotland lined up with Ethel Hay in goal, Rose Rayman at half-back, and Lilly St Clair up front. England had May Goodwin in goal, Mabel Bradbury at full-back, and Maud Starling at half-back. It was noted that the players dressed very suitably, and from a distance could not be distinguished from men. The Scotland team wore blue jerseys, white knickerbockers, red sashes, blue and white stockings, and blue and white cowls. England wore red jerseys, blue sashes, white knickerbockers, red and white stockings, and red and white cowls. The *Glasgow Herald* said both teams played in 'high-heeled boots'. Scotland won 3-0, but the *Bell's* match report was so dismissive it didn't even mention the score. 'The football shown was of the most primitive order,' it said, calling the match 'a humiliating spectacle'. The event had, however, attracted a large crowd, and a second match was arranged for the following week, this time in Glasgow, at Shawfield. Around 5,000 spectators turned up, and it was noted that none of them were 'of the fair sex'. The rowdy crowd made uncomplimentary remarks throughout the first half. Then, in the second half, hundreds of spectators charged onto the pitch and 'roughly jostled' the women, sending them fleeing back to their horse-drawn omnibus. Pitch invaders pulled up marker stakes and threw them at the bus, jeering as it made a hasty retreat. The players escaped with 'nothing more than serious fright'. Thankfully, the unpleasant incident didn't put an end to women's football in the Victorian era.

FOOTBALL IN IRELAND

The Irish Football Association was founded in 1880 by a group of mostly Belfast-based clubs led by Cliftonville – the country's oldest club. Cliftonville had been formed a year earlier by businessman John McCredy McAlery, and it was McAlery who arranged the meeting at the Queen's Park Hotel in Belfast at which the IFA was founded. The organisation's first president was Major Spencer Chichester, and McAlery was its first secretary. The IFA swiftly organised a challenge competition, which later became the Irish Cup. In the first final, in 1881, Moyola Park, from Castledawson in County Londonderry, beat Cliftonville 1-0. Irish clubs also participated in the 'English' FA Cup. Cliftonville reached the third round in 1886-87, but were thrashed 11-0 by another 'foreign' team – Partick Thistle. Linfield drew with Nottingham Forest in what was effectively the third round in 1888-89, but couldn't afford to travel for the replay and withdrew from the competition.

IRELAND BLOWN AWAY

Ireland's first international match was played at Bloomfield Road, Belfast, on 18 February 1882. It was bitterly cold, and a gale force wind was blowing rain and hail around the ground. The Irish players might have wished they had stayed indoors. Ireland were captained by John McAlery, and the side included 15-year-old forward Samuel Johnston and fleet-footed right-winger Billy McWha. But it was visitors England, led by Charles Bambridge, who dominated the game. *Bell's Life* called this 'an easy victory for England', and that was an understatement. England raced to a 5-0 half-time lead, scored eight more goals in the second half, and ended up winning 13-0. Howard Vaughton scored five, Arthur Brown scored four, Jimmy Brown got two, and Bambridge and Harry Cursham scored one each. Ireland's biggest ever defeat and England's biggest ever victory seems unlikely to be surpassed.

DOUBLE DISASTER

By 1882, England had played Scotland at international football 10 times and had won only twice. That record didn't befit a nation that purported to be the seat of association football, and the country's shortcomings were made abundantly clear in March 1882 when England lost again to Scotland, and then also to Wales, conceding a total of 10 goals, all within the space of three days. Despite having recently thrashed Ireland 13-0, this wasn't a vintage England team. Captained by Norman Bailey, its only real stars were Charles Bambridge and Billy Mosforth. At Hampden Park on 11 March, England were comprehensively beaten 5-1 by a Scotland team including George Ker, William Harrower and debutant Andrew Watson. Two days later, England were again 'doomed to defeat' against Wales. After leading 2-1 at half-time, England, who lost Bambridge to injury, suffered a complete collapse. Wales, captained by John Morgan, got four second half goals, including an own goal turned in by England's Alf Jones, and ran out 5-2 winners. The *Bell's Life* football columnist reacted angrily to England's defeats. '*That thing ill-got had ever bad success,*' he wrote, 'Shakespeare's words were brought painfully to my mind on receiving news of the double disaster which befell the English arms.' The selection committee was to blame, he said, in part for omitting so many 'leading Northerners': 'To my mind the whole system at present in vogue for the selection of the English teams needs a radical change.' The Scotland defeat could have been worse but for the performance of goalkeeper Harry 'Little Pilgrim' Swepstone. 'How many goals Swepstone saved, deponent knoweth not,' the columnist wrote. He also pointed an accusatory finger at the Scottish referee, penning a poem in his honour: 'Who gives offside? / Not I, said the Scotch ref / To all their appeals deaf / Always onside.' However, it was the defeat by relative newcomers to international football Wales that most annoyed the writer: 'The Scottish defeat was by no means unexpected. But to be beaten by Wales; this is, indeed, decadence.'

ANDREW WATSON

Full-back Andrew Watson played three times for Scotland between 1881 and 1882, and contemporary reports made no mention of his skin colour. Today, however, Watson is remembered as the first black international footballer. Born in British Guiana in 1857, Watson was the son of a wealthy Scottish sugar plantation owner and a British Guianan woman. He was sent to private school in London, and later studied at Glasgow University. After settling in Glasgow, he played for Queen's Park, and also became the club's secretary. Shortly before making his international debut, the Scottish FA Annual described Watson as, 'One of the very best backs we have; has great speed and tackles splendidly; powerful and sure kick; well worthy of a place in any representative team.' He made his international debut on 12 March 1881, and led his country to a 6-1 win over England. Watson also made appearances for English clubs Swifts and Corinthians. After football, Watson emigrated to Australia with his family. He died in Sydney in 1902, aged 44.

Queen's Park, 1881, Andrew Watson top left

99

NEWCASTLE UNITED

Originally known as Stanley FC, Newcastle United was formed in 1881 by a group of teenage friends from the Stanley Cricket Club, which played on a field at Stanley Street in Byker, to the east of Newcastle. The club's first captain was 18-year-old assistant teacher William Coulson. He scored in the club's first match – a 5-0 win over Elswick Leather Works. A couple of ground moves and a name change followed, before the club settled at Heaton Junction, in 1886, under the name East End FC. The club had cross-city rivals, West End, who played at a ground called St James' Park. Both were popular local clubs with keen fanbases, but East End gained prominence after influential secretary Tom Watson switched from West to East. Watson oversaw East End's entry into the FA Cup and Northern League competitions. Then, in 1892, West End went bust. East End took over the vacant lease at St James' Park, and moved to the heart of the city. In an attempt to dampen ill-feeling from fans, it was decided to change the club's name. East End became Newcastle United. The club played in red shirts, but switched to black and white stripes on election to the Football League second division in 1893. Newcastle played Woolwich Arsenal in a debut league match for both sides, and drew 2-2. The club won promotion to the first division in 1898, setting up a glorious Edwardian period during which Newcastle won three league titles and the FA Cup.

GREASY, MUDDY SLOPE

Newcastle United's St James' Park ground was initially regarded as 'most unsuitable to football'. 'Between goal and goal there is a most pronounced dip,' bemoaned the *Northern Echo*, 'and on Saturday the goal-mouth at the bottom end was nothing but a greasy, muddy slope of the most treacherous nature.' A visible slope, although no longer as greasy or muddy, still exists at St James' Park today.

CORINTHIANS

In 1882, the FA decided that England was at a disadvantage when it played Scotland at football. Scotland's dominance in international matches was attributed to the fact that its team was based almost entirely around players from one club – Queen's Park. The Scottish players were familiar with each other, and were more easily able to develop the 'combination' teamwork the national side was famed for. It was decided that England needed a club that could similarly act as a feeder team for the country's national side. That club was Corinthian FC, or the Corinthians. The chief administrator behind the Corinthians was FA assistant secretary Nicholas Lane Jackson. Known to his players as 'Pa', Jackson was a staunch advocate of amateur football, and the Corinthians remained steadfastly amateur, even after professionalism was legalised. Over the next few years Jackson assembled an all-star amateur side, cherry-picking the best players from leading teams. Because the Corinthians didn't compete in the FA Cup, or latterly in the Football League, amateurs could continue to play for their old clubs and become a Corinthian. And there was a big incentive for them – an England cap. Within a few years of the club's formation, the England team was comprised almost entirely of Corinthians. This had a mixed effect. England's results against Scotland did improve, but many very talented professionals were overlooked. Pa Jackson would have argued that his amateurs were better players than the professionals, and the Corinthians did beat several top professional sides in friendly matches. Jackson and his Corinthians lost their influence over the national team in the mid-1890s, although top amateurs such as Charles Wreford-Brown and GO Smith continued to play for, and captain, England. Jackson quit the FA in 1897, disillusioned by the growth of professionalism. The Corinthians subsequently became a touring side, acting as football missionaries to Europe, South Africa, and Brazil. It was a visit of the English amateurs to São Paolo in 1910 that inspired the creation of Brazil's Corinthians football club.

OLD BOYS BEATEN

The 1883 FA Cup final represented a changing of the football guard. Blackburn Olympic was a working class club from the north. In the 11 seasons that the FA Cup had existed, it had only previously been won by gentlemen's sides made up of public school old boys. Olympic captain Jack Warburton was a plumber, Jimmy Costley worked in a cotton mill, and Arthur Matthews was a picture-framer. By contrast, the Old Etonians team was exactly what it said on the tin. Captained by Arthur Kinnaird, the side included the aristocratic likes of Harry Goodhart and Percy de Paravicini. Olympic had beaten Druids and Old Carthusians to reach the final, but were still underdogs against the reigning cup holders. However, Olympic had a secret weapon in the shape of England international half-back Jack Hunter. The former Sheffield man now ran a pub in Blackburn, and occupied a kind of player-coach role at Olympic. Hunter decided to do something that no other FA Cup finalist had ever done before, and he took the team to Blackpool for several days of actual training. This was completely unheard of at the time, and critics argued too much preparation would tire the players out. But Hunter's training regime, coupled with his innovative 2-3-5 formation, saw Olympic well. 8,000 turned up to watch the match at the Oval. 'Perhaps on no former occasion have more spectators been present, and all the cognoscenti were at the fore,' reported *the Graphic*. Old Etonians took the lead through Goodhart in the first half, but Olympic equalised through Matthews in the second. It was a bruising and exhausting match, and, with the score level after 90 minutes, it went to extra time. By this point, the Etonians were pretty much a spent force. Olympic took advantage, and Costley scored their winner. Travelling fans, and those in Blackburn who had followed the match via telegraph, were able to celebrate as the cup was presented to Warburton. 'It'll never go back to London,' he said. That cup never did – it was stolen in 1895. More importantly, the public school old boys' FA Cup monopoly had been broken.

BRITISH HOME CHAMPIONSHIP

The British Home Championship (BHC), the first international football tournament, began in 1884. It was contested between the four British home nations – England, Ireland, Scotland, and Wales – and took a league format. The first tournament kicked off in January 1884. Both England and Scotland beat Ireland and Wales, and what was effectively the deciding match took place between England and Scotland on 16 March 1884. Scotland won a tight match 1-0 courtesy of a John Smith goal, and went on to claim the first BHC title. Only England and Scotland won the BHC during the Victorian era, and the balance of power was fairly even. Scotland won eight titles to England's seven, and the two nations shared the title twice. The BHC continued to be played for 100 years, through to 1984.

BHC WINNERS

1884	Scotland
1885	Scotland
1886	England/Scotland shared
1887	Scotland
1888	England
1889	Scotland
1890	England/Scotland shared
1891	England
1892	England
1893	England
1894	Scotland
1895	England
1896	Scotland
1897	Scotland
1898	England
1899	England
1900	Scotland

SCOTCH PROFESSORS

The influx of Scottish footballers into the English game began in the late 1870s. The first Scottish import is thought to have been James 'Reddie' Lang, a Glasgow shipyard worker who had lost the sight in one eye during an accident at the yard. Despite this apparent disadvantage, muscular forward Lang played with distinction for Clydesdale and Third Lanark, and became a Scottish international. He also represented Glasgow in matches against Sheffield, where in 1876 he came to the attention of the Wednesday. Lang was offered a factory job by a Wednesday director, and moved to Sheffield. He later admitted that his 'job' mainly involved reading the newspaper, and that he had not crossed the border to play for nothing. Lang was quite possibly football's first ever professional. Other Scottish players soon followed Lang to English football. James Love and Fergus Suter joined Darwen from Partick Thistle. Blackburn Rovers signed Scottish internationals Jimmy Douglas and Hugh McIntyre. By the early 1880s, English clubs were placing advertisements in Scottish newspapers, inviting players for trials. And Scottish players weren't only valued for their skills. English clubs wanted their tactical know-how, too. The Scottish combination game was far superior to the English dribbling game, as evidenced by Scotland's dominance of international matches at the time. Scottish football was considered to be 'scientific', and imported players were dubbed 'Scotch professors'. They were brought in to play and to teach – with the expectation that they would reveal to their English teammates the secrets of Scottish football. Many Scotch professors were installed as captains of their new teams. The value of Scottish imports was most evidently demonstrated at Preston North End. Jack Ross, Geordie Drummond and David Russell were among the cross-border acquisitions that helped the Preston 'Invincibles' become the most successful club of the mid-1880s. Sunderland also benefited, building their league-winning 'team of all talents' around Scotch professors.

KICKED OUT

In January 1884, Preston North End played Upton Park in an FA Cup fourth round tie that changed football forever. The match was played at Deepdale in front of up to 15,000 spectators, with anticipation having been raised by press coverage regarding the alleged professionalism of Preston's imported Scotch professors. The Preston side, including revolutionary Scottish imports Jack Ross and Geordie Drummond, as well as local star Fred Dewhurst, were firm favourites, and they took an early lead. However, a second half equaliser for Segar Bastard's fiercely amateur Upton Park took the match into extra time. Preston scored what they thought was a worthy winner, only to have the goal disallowed. The tie ended as a draw, but it would never be replayed. On the following day, it was widely reported in the press that Upton Park had lodged a protest against Preston on the grounds of professionalism. Key Upton Park figures denied they had protested – and in fact offered Preston their support. Nevertheless, the protest was heard at an FA meeting on the following Saturday. Here it transpired that, several weeks earlier, FA assistant secretary (and leading advocate of the amateur game) Pa Jackson had obtained evidence that Preston had recently 'enticed' two players – Sandy Roberston and James Ferguson – from Scotland. On considering the evidence, it was decided that Preston had broken the FA's rule 15, which stated: 'Any member of a club receiving remuneration or consideration of any sort above his actual expenses and any wages lost by any such player taking part in any match shall be debarred from taking part in either cup, inter-association, or international contests, and any club employing such a player shall be excluded from this association.' The FA committee, chaired by Francis Marindin, expelled Preston from the FA Cup, but stopped short of kicking them out of the association. Although the FA remained dead against professionalism, the power and popularity of clubs that embraced it could no longer be ignored. It was clear that football was about to undergo a major change.

PROFESSIONALISM

As football's popularity grew, professionalism became inevitable. Football was now a business, and footballers were a commodity. Professionalism remained illegal, but it was well-known that many clubs were making veiled payments. The 'Scotch professors' imported by English clubs were not crossing the border purely for the love of football. They were being offered undemanding employment at local firms, time off to play football, inflated expenses, and – in some cases – illicit signing-on and match fees. They were being paid to play football. Two key incidents forced the issue of professionalism into the open. The first was the punishment of the Sheffield 'Zulu' team, which had received payments for exhibition matches. The second was the expulsion of Preston North End from the 1883-84 FA Cup. CW Alcock recognised that football was changing, and he proposed that professionalism should be legalised. However, at a packed FA meeting in February 1884, only three out of around 200 delegates supported Alcock's proposal. Instead, a committee was set up to investigate 'the existence of veiled professionalism and the importation of players' and repress these 'serious evils' and 'abuses'. The issue threatened to split the FA. At a further meeting in January 1885, with 25 clubs threatening to quit and form their own professional association, Alcock argued that it was impossible to continue to operate football 'on strictly amateur lines'. There were 113 votes in support of legalising professionalism, and 108 against. The FA required a two-thirds majority for a motion to be carried, so the affair rolled on. Finally, in July 1885, at a meeting of just 47 delegates that lasted only a few minutes, an agreement was reached. Professionals would be allowed to play in cup matches provided they met the qualification criteria of 'birth or residence for two years last past within six miles of the ground or headquarters of the club for which they play'. It was a compromise, but professionalism had been legalised. The 'birth or residence' restriction was eventually removed in 1889.

NEVILL 'NUTS' COBBOLD

William Nevill Cobbold, known as Nevill, or 'Nuts', was regarded as 'the most individually brilliant dribbler' ever seen. A vicar's son, Cobbold attended Charterhouse and Cambridge, and played football for Old Carthusians, Cambridge University, and – most notably – the Corinthians. He also played nine times for England between 1883 and 1887, and scored six international goals. Devastatingly quick and possessing a fierce shot, Cobbold could terrify opponents. However, as brilliant as he may have been at running with the ball, he steadfastly refused to head it – and he wasn't keen on passing it, either. Nevertheless, Victorian historian Montague Shearman said Cobbold was 'the best type of forward player'. Former England captain GO Smith said, 'I put him first among all the forwards I have known.' And FA president William Pickford named Cobbold as one of the three greatest forwards of all time. A schoolteacher by profession, Cobbold also wrote and published poetry. Born in 1862, he died in 1922.

BON ACCORD

On 12 September 1885, the first round of the Scottish Cup provided one of the most incredible football results of all time. In fact, it provided *two* of the most incredible football results of all time. The first was a result that remains familiar to football fans around the world – Arbroath 36-0 Bon Accord. Poor Bon Accord shouldn't even have been playing in the cup. They were actually a cricket club – Orion CC, from Aberdeen. A mix-up saw them mistakenly invited to enter the cup instead of Orion FC – an unrelated club, also from Aberdeen. The cricketers adopted the name 'Bon Accord' (a watchword associated with the storming of Aberdeen Castle during the wars of independence) and set off to face Arbroath – an experienced cup team. It was obvious that the newcomers were going to get a thrashing, but what happened was even more remarkable than could have been predicted. Bon Accord were 15-0 down by half-time. 'The Aberdonians might as well have been outside the ropes for the resistance that they provided,' said the *Scottish Athletic Journal*. By full-time, it was 36-0, with 18-year-old Arbroath forward John Petrie scoring 13 times. 'The leather was landed between the posts 41 times, but five of the times were disallowed,' reported the *Journal*. 'Here and there, enthusiasts would be seen, scoring sheet and pencil in hand, taking note of the goals as one would score runs at a cricket match.' In fact, referee Dave Stormont later remembered disallowing seven goals. Arbroath goalkeeper Jim Milne never touched the ball, while poor Andrew Lornie, the Bon Accord keeper, was constantly busy retrieving it. Amazingly, in another Scottish Cup tie on the very same day, Dundee Harp beat Aberdeen Rovers 35-0. The referee thought there had been 37 goals, but Harp's secretary sportingly argued that he had only seen 35, and the lower score was recorded. The secretary would come to regret that. Harp's players and officials thought they had chalked up a record score, only to find out, several hours later, that it had been eclipsed. 36-0 remains the biggest ever scoreline in British football history.

INTERNATIONAL BOARD

The first meeting of the International Football Association Board (IFAB) took place in London on 2 June 1886. It had been decided that the English, Irish, Scottish, and Welsh Football Associations should form a joint board in order that the Laws of the Game could be administered by a single body. Each country would share a common set of laws, and any changes to those laws would need to be approved unanimously. The IFAB would also discuss 'generally any matters affecting association football in its international relations'. The first major law change agreed upon prevented goalkeepers from handling the ball in their opponent's half of the field. By the end of the Victorian era, the IFAB had defined the offside rule, introduced penalty kicks, and set out many other laws that still exist today. The IFAB still controls the Laws of the Game, but it has another member – FIFA joined in 1913.

STANDING ON THE LINE

The recorded result of an 1887 match between Saltburn Swifts and Stockton St Peter's was 1-0 to Saltburn. But Stockton's RT Johnson was left aggrieved – and complained to the *Northern Echo* newspaper. The match had been played at Saltburn in high winds and descending darkness. 'We could not see the goal-posts a dozen yards off,' wrote Johnson. But his main gripe was with the Saltburn fans. 'They were all standing on the goal-line, and we were scrimmaging round the goal the whole time, and had the ball through repeatedly, but they kicked it back, and if we said anything they merely laughed.' Johnson also accused the Saltburn goalkeeper of kicking the ball away. 'The wind carried it about a mile, and it took five or 10 minutes to bring it back,' he wrote. 'We claim the match a draw – one goal each.' The *Echo*'s football columnist showed little sympathy. 'It took five or 10 minutes to bring it back!' he responded. 'This is too good! Bring down the curtain!'

THE OVAL

The most prestigious football ground of the Victorian era was the Oval, then known as the Kennington Oval, in South London. Then, as now, it was actually a cricket ground, and the home of Surrey County Cricket Club. It just so happened that the secretary of Surrey CCC was one CW Alcock – also the secretary of the Wanderers club and soon to be the secretary of the FA. It was thanks to Alcock that Wanderers made the Oval their semi-permanent home ground in 1869. The club went on to play more than 150 games at the ground. The Oval also played host to the 'Alcock Internationals' between 1870 and 1872. The first of these unofficial England versus Scotland contests attracted around 400 spectators - typical at that time for a high profile football match, but nothing compared to the 20,000 that international cricket matches could attract. 'Official' international matches were played at the Oval from March 1873, and they attracted more substantial crowds. 2,500 attended the 1873 England versus Scotland match. Around the same number paid a shilling each to attend the first FA Cup final, between Wanderers and Royal Engineers in 1872. The football ground was set up to the north of the cricket pitch. The Oval's ground had two 'ends' – the Crown Baths End and the Gasometer End. The Crown Baths was a private swimming pool that occasionally hosted water polo matches. The Gasometer End was so-named because it was – and still is – famously overlooked by a large gas holder. 20 FA Cup finals plus two replays were played at the Oval through to 1892. Gates increased from 6,500 in 1882 to 22,000 in 1889. The current pavilion – built in 1888 – helped extend the ground's capacity, and the 1892 final drew a massive crowd of almost 33,000 spectators. After that, however, Surrey CCC decided that it could no longer allow football to damage its wickets. The final was moved to Fallowfield Stadium in Manchester and Goodison Park in Liverpool, before finding a new permanent venue at the Crystal Palace. Football's most famous venue, Wembley Stadium, wasn't built until 1923.

International match (rugby) at the Oval, 1872

CROSSBAR CHALLENGE

In the winter of 1887-88, an FA Cup fourth round replay between Crewe Alexandra and Swifts was ordered to be re-played again due to an argument over a crossbar. The initial match was played at Crewe, and an end-to-end game finished as a 2-2 draw. However, tempers were high, with Swifts claiming Crewe had played 'none too fair a game'. The replay, at the Oval on the following Saturday involved 'some very exciting play', and the Swifts triumphed 3-2. However, Crewe subsequently lodged an appeal with the FA, claiming that one of the crossbars was a full two inches lower than the required height. The FA duly ordered another replay, two weeks later, at the neutral venue of the County Ground in Derby. In unfavourable conditions, the game was 'by no means a brilliant one'. Crewe had an early goal disallowed for offside (although 'some of the spectators avowed that the umpire was mistaken'), but eventually won 2-1. Swifts went out, and Crewe went through – eventually reaching the semi-final.

In the early days of association football, newspaper coverage was sparse. 'Newspapers, as a whole, took very little notice of matches,' recalled journalist Jimmy Catton. 'The reports were brief, and there were none of the personal paragraphs, garrulous items, and more or less sensational news which are now part not only of weekly periodicals, but of morning and evening newspapers.' National dailies virtually ignored football, leaving it to weeklies such as *Bell's Life* and the *Athletic News*, and to regional newspapers in prominent football areas. Even then, football would have to vie for column space with other sports such as horse racing, pedestrianism, and quoits. Early match reports were typically submitted by club secretaries, and were formal and perfunctory – and often biased and unreliable. It wasn't until the football boom of the 1880s that newspapers began to take the game seriously – following the realisation that coverage of the popular sport increased sales. Reporters were sent to cover matches, and columnists wrote opinion pieces and solicited correspondence. Team selection, foul play, and disallowed goals were among the many subjects debated in newspaper columns. Football columnists often wrote under pen names, such as 'Off-Side', 'Goal-Post', or 'Spectator'. For fans unable to attend matches in person, newspapers provided a way to follow their teams. Initially, readers would have to wait until Monday for details of Saturday afternoon matches. Carrier pigeons and telegraph boys were used to ferry scores around the country, and fans would gather at local newspaper offices for updates from away matches. The installation of telegraph poles at grounds from the mid-1880s meant reports could be filed more quickly, and allowed the publication of Saturday night football specials. Early football writing was often flowery, and littered with high-brow references, although it became more populist as football developed into the working man's game. Crucially, journalism played an important role in nurturing and promoting the game in its formative years.

JIMMY CATTON

JAH 'Jimmy' Catton, better known to his readers as 'Tityrus', was the most important and influential football journalist of the Victorian era. Born in 1860, Catton began his career as a teenager at the *Preston Herald*. His rise to prominence coincided with that of Preston North End – a club with which he was enthusiastically involved. At only 4ft 10in tall, Catton was no footballer, but he had an informed and passionate eye for the game. He began to submit match reports to the Manchester-based *Athletic News*, and became a full-time reporter for the paper. Within a few years, he was appointed editor. With Catton onboard, the *Athletic News* became the most popular football paper in the country. Catton was a pioneer of 'new journalism', injecting opinion and colour into football coverage. It was common to write under pen names, and Catton took his from Greek mythology. 'Tityrus' became a popular and respected figure among players and spectators alike. Catton's career encompassed the evolution of the football reporter. In the days before press boxes he would wander the touch-line or stand behind the goal-posts. Later, wooden benches or desks were placed at the touch-line for the benefit of reporters. 'There was no shelter, and when the day of telegraphing reports arrived the telegraphic forms were often wet through, and sometimes blown away,' he said. 'Many a time I have left a match with clothes saturated by rain and with marrow chilled.' Although he had a strong reputation for impartiality, Catton retained an affection for Preston. In 1897, as Aston Villa celebrated winning the double, Catton 'rashly remarked' that it was a shame his beloved Preston had been deprived of their unique double-winning record. 'The Villa players naturally objected to this observation,' remembered Catton. 'The discussion became heated and even reached the stage of a threat to drop me out of the window. The "Villains" relented and repented when they looked me up and down and considered my miniature proportions in relation to my daring.' Catton died in 1936, aged 76.

FOOTBALL NEWSPAPERS

Athletic News (1875-1931)
This Manchester-based journal of amateur sport evolved into the leading national football paper of the Victorian era, under the editorships of JJ Bentley and Jimmy Catton (AKA Tityrus).

Bell's Life in London, and Sporting Chronicle (1822-86)
The first general newspaper to give prominent coverage to sport, *Bell's* flourished during football's formative years due to its focus on the increasingly-popular game.

The Field, or Country Gentleman's Newspaper (1853-date)
Still published today, the *Field* was instrumental in the football rules debate. Aimed at a higher-class of reader, its football coverage initially focussed on public school games.

The Goal: The Chronicle of Football (1873-74)
Published by a Mr EM Fraser of London, this was referred to by Jimmy Catton as 'surely the very first of football papers'.

Saturday Night (1882-98)
This Birmingham evening weekly was the first 'football special', beginning a popular tradition of Saturday pink 'uns and green 'uns that remained popular for a hundred years.

Sporting Chronicle (1880-1931)
This Manchester-based sister publication of the *Athletic News* was an early outlet for the football writing of Jimmy Catton.

Sporting Life (1859-1998)
Launched as a direct rival to *Bell's Life*, this paper concentrated on horse racing, but also provided daily football news.

The Sportsman (1865-1924)
CW Alcock began his journalism career at this paper, which also published football guides and annuals.

BLACKGUARDLY AND DISGRACEFUL

In 1887, the *Northern Echo* printed an alarming yet undeniably amusing letter from Cleveland referee John Reed Jnr describing a match between Yarm and North Skelton that had resulted in 'the most blackguardly and disgraceful scenes ever witnessed on a football field'. North Skelton won 8-3, much to the chagrin of Yarm fans and players. 'Every score made by the visitors was appealed against on the grounds of offside,' said Reed, 'and as the two umpires systematically disagreed, the onus of deciding against these appeals rested entirely with me.' As the goals stacked up, the crowd became increasingly aggrieved: 'The first and second goals given to North Skelton caused some grumbling, the third and fourth ignited a blaze of indignation, the fourth and fifth produced hoots and yells, and so on until the eighth goal was got, when the Yarm people were dancing madly.' Things really kicked off at full-time. 'After blowing the whistle I walked smartly away from the crowd,' said Reed. 'It would have been foolhardy to have gone to it. For a minute all was quiet. Then horrible yells rained from the sky.' Reed was confronted by a 'panting and cursing' spectator who 'used very violent language, which, summed up, meant he wanted to kill me'. Then he was attacked, 'like red Indians at the charge', by 'a couple of hundred reckless hobbledehoys and half-drunken men'. 'Quickly throwing my overcoat into the face of the first assailant as a feint, the next instant I took to the open country at top speed,' he said. 'The situation was intensely funny. Here I was speeding down the valley from the unrighteous of Yarm. If I had been caught, it might have been the opposite of funny. The intent was to put poor me in the river. But, as the evening was cold and frosty, naturally there was an objection on my part. If I had no fear, I certainly had the wings that fear lends, and I soon lost the foes, and gained the shelter of a kind and friendly house.' The Cleveland FA instructed their secretary to take legal action against Mr Reed's assailants. It is unknown whether or not he got his overcoat back.

TOTTENHAM HOTSPUR

Hotspur FC was formed in 1882 as an offshoot of the Hotspur Cricket Club by schoolboys who attended the All Hallows Church in Tottenham. Harry 'Hotspur' Percy was the Earl of Northumberland, whose exploits were fictionalised in Shakespeare's *Henry IV Part 1*. But there was already a Hotspur FC, in Wimbledon, so the club changed its name to Tottenham Hotspur in 1884. The first kit was a navy jersey, with a red shield bearing the letter 'H' on the right breast. After several changes, the club settled on white shirts from 1898. Tottenham joined the Southern League and turned professional in 1895. The club's first manager was Frank Brettell. Among the players Brettell signed was former Everton forward John Cameron, who would soon replace Brettell as player-manager. The 'Hotspurs' moved to White Hart Lane in 1899, and won the Southern League in 1900 under Cameron's stewardship.

FA CUFF

The first round of the 1887-88 FA Cup tournament produced several high-scoring results. Sheffield Heeley beat Attercliffe 9-0, Notts Rangers beat Jardines 10-1, and Accrington beat Rossendale 11-0. Blackburn Rovers were 10-0 up at Bury when the match was declared a walkover. But the most remarkable result occurred at Deepdale, where Preston North End beat Hyde 26-0. 'A most one-sided game,' remarked the *London Standard*. Preston were 12 goals up by half-time, despite the best efforts of Hyde goalkeeper Charles Bunyan, who was described as 'a clinking good opponent'. Hyde lost centre-half Bowers to injury, but were sympathetically allowed to bring on a substitute. Nevertheless, there were 14 more goals in the second half. Jimmy Ross scored seven, Jack Gordon got five, Sam Thomson scored four, and Fred Dewhurst got three. George Drummond and Johnny Graham both scored two, and Nick Ross, David Russell and John Goodall got one goal each.

CARD KING

Football cards were first issued in 1887 by Bradford toy shop owner John Baines. The self-styled 'Football Card King' operated from a dolls' hospital on Bradford's North Parade, and distributed his cards from a brightly-painted carriage pulled by a horse with a monkey on its back. The small shield-shaped cards featured colourful depictions of teams and kits, and sometimes drawings of popular players. Baines created demand for his products via ingenious promotions, including hidden gold medal cards that could be exchanged for prizes. Eager Victorian kids would queue outside confectioners for new deliveries in an effort to get hold of the latest cards. Kids traded them via a card-flicking game known as 'skaging', with the winner taking all. Inevitably, as the popularity of Baines cards soared, competitors arrived, notably from WN Sharpe, also from Bradford, who produced a huge range of 'Play Up!' cards featuring hundreds of different teams and players. Tobacco companies also began to produce football cards. The first set of football cigarette cards was produced in 1896 by Manchester firm Marcus & Co. The 'Footballers and Club Colours' collection is now extremely rare and valuable.

COMIC READS

Illustrated comics and serials were all the rage in the late 19th century, and football was a popular subject matter. Comics such as *Fun* and *Funny Folk* published cartoons highlighting the humorous side of football, and young Victorians were gripped by football serials that appeared in magazines like *Big Budget* and the *Boys of England Journal*. The king of the football serial was Maxwell Scott, the author of such potboilers as *Stolen: The English Cup!*, *The Goalkeeper's Revenge*, and *The Missing Forward*. Comics also promoted football tournaments for readers, such as the *Big Budget* Football Cup, which offered winners a 'grand-looking' silver cup and 'handsome' medals.

BAD PENNY

A failed attempt to con a football ground gateman was related by the *Newcastle Courant* in September 1888. 'Apropos of the football rage, the following incident can be vouched for,' the paper explained. 'At a recent match at Sunderland a youth tendered a bad threepenny piece, which escaped the vigilant eyes of the gateman, and the youth was admitted. A minute afterwards, a companion who had just entered the field went up to the youth afore-mentioned, and, in a melancholy voice, said, "Look here, I have just been taken in, for I gave the gatekeeper sixpence, and got back the bad threepenny bit as change."'

UNNECESSARY ROUGHNESS

Long after football was codified, rough play, injuries, and even fatalities remained a problem. The 1888-89 season was considered particularly dangerous, with reports of eight fatalities and numerous serious injuries across all levels of the game. 'There is no denying that unnecessary roughness has crept into football,' commented the *Pall Mall Gazette*, 'and while we cherish no idea that it can be reduced to a parlour pastime, there is no reason why it should sink to the level of the modern substitute for prizefighting.' The paper urged the FA to clamp down on rough play for the good of the future of the game. 'When men stout of heart quail, and to their fears are added the entreaties of wives, mothers, sisters, and aunts, no wonder that there have been instances of celebrated players packing up their jerseys and closing their football career.' There followed a long list of fatalities and injuries, including a dislocated spine, brain fever, lockjaw, limb amputations, fractured collar bones, broken legs, a ruptured kidney, two dislocated knees, and a broken nose. 'We have no wish to be sensational, but rather practical,' said the paper, adding that the FA must not 'shut their eyes' to the situation.

ARTHUR WHARTON

Ghana-born Arthur Wharton came to England in 1882 to train as a missionary, but soon abandoned that path in favour of sport. Wharton, who once held the world record for the 100-yard dash, first played football as a winger for Darlington, until his wayward kicking saw him converted to a goalkeeper. He shone in his new position – 'There is not another man who can keep goal with half his ability,' wrote the *Northern Echo*. Wharton moved to Preston North End in 1886, becoming the first black professional footballer. He developed a reputation for clowning around, and would often hang from and sit on his crossbar. This may have been an attempt to ingratiate himself with racist spectators. 'Is the darkie's pate too thick for it to dawn upon him that between the posts is no place for a skylark?' wrote the *Athletic News*. Wharton was dropped by Preston, and moved to Rotherham, and then Sheffield United. A spectator recalled a remarkable save he made for Rotherham: 'I saw Wharton jump, take hold of the crossbar, catch the ball between his legs, and cause three onrushing forwards to fall into the net.' A football pioneer, Wharton didn't receive proper recognition until after his death. Having struggled with alcoholism, he died in a sanatorium in 1930.

FOOTBALL LEAGUE

The world's first professional football league competition was founded in March 1888 by Aston Villa director William McGregor. The aim was to provide professional clubs with a reliable revenue stream away from FA Cup and friendly matches. The league was formed at a meeting at Anderson's Hotel in London on the eve of the 1888 FA Cup final, and its rules and regulations were hammered out over a series of subsequent meetings in Manchester and Birmingham. McGregor, a Scot who owned a drapery business in Aston, was appointed league president, and Harry Lockett of Stoke was appointed secretary. It was agreed that fixtures should not clash with FA Cup ties. Teams would play each other home and away, and two points would be awarded for a win and one point for a draw. Goal difference would not be taken into account. 12 clubs from the Midlands and the North of England signed up as founder members. Three other clubs (Nottingham Forest, Sheffield Wednesday and Halliwell Rovers) were refused admission as it was thought that there wasn't room for extra fixtures in the calendar. The first winners of the Football League were Preston North End – the Invincibles – who remained unbeaten throughout the season and finished 11 points clear of second-placed Aston Villa. Stoke (later renamed Stoke City) finished bottom. Preston's John Goodall was the league's first top scorer, with 21 goals. Preston won the league again in its second season (but were no longer invincible – they lost four matches). Everton, Sheffield United, Sunderland (three times) and Aston Villa (four times) also won the league in the Victorian era. The Football League added a second division in 1892, and by 1900 had expanded to include 36 teams. All but one of the 12 original Football League clubs still exist today. The exception is Accrington FC (not to be confused with Accrington Stanley), who resigned from the league in 1893 following relegation to the second division, and folded in 1896.

FIRST FOOTBALL LEAGUE TABLE, 1888-89

	P	W	D	L	F	A	Pts
Preston North End	**22**	**18**	**4**	**0**	**74**	**15**	**40**
Aston Villa	22	12	5	5	61	43	29
Wolves	22	12	4	6	50	37	28
Blackburn Rovers	22	10	6	6	66	45	26
Bolton Wanderers	22	10	2	10	63	59	22
West Bromwich Albion	22	10	2	10	40	46	22
Accrington	22	6	8	8	48	48	20
Everton	22	9	2	11	35	46	20
Burnley	22	7	3	12	42	62	17
Derby County	22	7	2	13	41	61	16
Notts County	22	5	2	15	40	73	12
Stoke FC	22	4	4	14	26	51	12

ANOTHER FOOTBALL LEAGUE

In April 1888, just weeks after the formation of the Football League, a rival league came into existence. Named the Football Combination, it was substantially less successful. The Combination was founded by a group of disgruntled clubs who believed that the Football League wasn't representative of the interests of English football. Founding members included Blackburn Olympic, Bootle, Burslem Port Vale, Crewe Alexandra, Darwen, Derby Midland, Grimsby Town, Haliwell, Leek, Lincoln City, Long Eaton Rangers, Notts Rangers, Newton Heath, Northwich Victoria, Small Heath Alliance, Walsall Town Swifts, and Witton. It was agreed that, rather than being organised centrally, fixtures would be arranged directly between individual clubs. Unsurprisingly, this didn't work, and the Combination folded before its first season could be completed.

NORTHERN LEAGUE

Founded just 12 months after the Football League, in 1889, the Northern League is the world's second oldest league competition. Based in the North East of England, it was formed to cater for that region's many clubs that had been overlooked by the initially Midlands and North West-based Football League. Won in its first season by Darlington St Augustine's, the competition was then briefly dominated by Middlesbrough Ironopolis. The 'Nops' only existed for five years, but won the Northern League three times, played in two FA Cup quarter-finals, and won election to the Football League, where they played a single season before resigning and being disbanded. Other Victorian-era Northern League winners included Middlesbrough, Darlington, Stockton, and Bishop Auckland. Newcastle United also played in the Northern League before being elected to the Football League.

SOUTHERN LEAGUE

Formed in 1895, founder members of the Southern League included Millwall Athletic (now just Millwall), Luton Town, Reading and Swindon Town. Southampton St Mary's (now Southampton), Tottenham Hotspur and Queen's Park Rangers were among other high-profile sides that joined the league in its early years. Millwall won the first two league seasons, and then Southampton won the next three. Tottenham won the last league of the Victorian era, in the 1899-1900 season.

FOOTBALL ALLIANCE

Another rival to the Football League, the Football Alliance was formed in 1889 by clubs including Crewe Alexandra, Darwen, Grimsby Town, Newton Heath, and Small Heath. The Alliance lasted three seasons, during which it was won by the Wednesday, Stoke and Nottingham Forest, before being integrated into the Football League as a second division.

FOOTBALL LEAGUE WINNERS

Season	Winner	Runner-up
1888–89	Preston North End	Aston Villa
1889–90	Preston North End	Everton
1890–91	Everton	Preston North End
1891–92	Sunderland	Preston North End
1892–93	Sunderland	Preston North End
1893–94	Aston Villa	Sunderland
1894–95	Sunderland	Everton
1895–96	Aston Villa	Derby County
1896–97	Aston Villa	Sheffield United
1897–98	Sheffield United	Sunderland
1898–99	Aston Villa	Liverpool
1899–1900	Aston Villa	Sheffield United

FOOTBALL LEAGUE TOP GOALSCORERS

Season	Player (Club)	
1888–89	John Goodall (Preston North End)	21
1889–90	Jimmy Ross (Preston North End)	24
1890–91	Jack Southworth (Blackburn Rovers)	26
1891–92	John Campbell I (Sunderland)	32
1892–93	John Campbell I (Sunderland)	31
1893–94	Jack Southworth (Everton)	27
1894–95	John Campbell I (Sunderland)	22
1895–96	John Campbell II (Aston Villa)	20
	Steve Bloomer (Derby County)	20
1896–97	Steve Bloomer (Derby County)	22
1897–98	Fred Wheldon (Aston Villa)	21
1898–99	Steve Bloomer (Derby County)	23
1899–1900	Billy Garraty (Aston Villa)	27

REJECTED LEAGUE CLUBS

As the Football League became established, the regular income its fixtures brought in became increasingly important. Clubs needed to apply for election to the league, and hope to gain sufficient votes for admittance. Several clubs applied for election without success during the Victorian era:

Ashton North End: From Ashton-under-Lyne in Lancashire, 'the Onions' applied for Football League status in 1899. They folded and never played again after their rejection.

Chorley: The club still exists today, playing in the Northern Premier League, and it could have been a Football League club had it managed to achieve enough votes in 1899.

Fairfield Athletic: This Greater Manchester Club made three attempts at election to the league, but, despite winning more votes than Tottenham, was rejected, and subsequently folded.

Liverpool Caledonians: This team of Scottish Merseysiders had barely played a match when it applied for election in 1892, and only played a handful more following rejection.

Birmingham St George's: Refused election following the first Football League season, this club briefly played in the Alliance, before financial problems snuffed it out of existence.

Rossendale: From Rawtenstall, in Lancashire's Rossendale Valley, Rossendale competed in the FA Cup, and were briefly one of the most high-profile clubs in the Lancashire League. But no votes meant no election in 1894 and the club folded in 1897. A new club, Rossendale United, formed in 1898.

South Shore: This Blackpool side failed to get elected in 1889, but eventually made it to the Football League after an 1899 merger with local rivals Blackpool FC.

Sunderland Albion: Northern League side Albion applied for election in 1890, but lost out to local rivals Sunderland AFC. There were three failed bids in all, and Albion folded in 1892.

Wigan County: Not to be confused with Wigan Athletic, County formed in 1897, failed to win election to the Football League in 1899, and folded in 1900.

PRESTON NORTH END

Known as 'The Invincibles', Preston North End were one of the most formidable and influential sides of the Victorian era. Formed as a cricket club in 1863, Preston also played rugby before turning to association football. The club played its first football match in 1878, and made a permanent switch to football in 1881. The man behind the switch was club chairman Billy Sudell, the manager of the local Goodair cotton mills, who was described as 'the life and spirit of the North End'. In March 1881, Preston were thrashed 16-0 by Blackburn Rovers. But improvement was swift. It came after Sudell made a conscious decision to turn Preston into a professional side. Although professionalism was still illegal, the illicit payment of players was widespread throughout the game. Sudell began to recruit talented Scottish players, or 'Scotch professors', offering them lucrative jobs, plus match fees. With Glasgow having already been plundered by English clubs, Sudell went to Edinburgh, signing Heart of Midlothian captain Nick Ross, and Geordie Drummond from St Bernard's. John Goodall was signed from nearby Great Lever. Another signing, Fred Dewhurst, was a local schoolteacher. In January 1884, Preston were kicked out of the FA Cup competition for paying professionals. However, the incident provoked a discussion that led to the legalisation of professionalism in the following year. That, in turn, led to the formation of the Football League, of which Preston were founder members. And, in the first league season of 1888-89, Preston won the league and cup double without losing a single match – thus earning the 'Invincibles' tag. The club won the league again in 1889-90, although not invincibly. After that, however, the club's fortunes declined. The great Nick Ross was forced to retire due to ill health in 1893, and he died in the following year. Team captain Fred Dewhurst died shortly afterwards. Then, in 1895, Billy Sudell was imprisoned for embezzling funds from the cotton mills to pay his players. The era of the Invincibles was over.

THE INVINCIBLES

The Preston North End 'Invincibles' squad that won the Football League and FA Cup double in 1888-89:

Name	Pos	Nat	Apps	Goals
James Trainer*	GK	Wal	20	0
Bob Howarth	FB	Eng	23	0
Bob Holmes	FB	Eng	26	1
Sandy Robertson*	HB	Sco	22	3
David Russell	HB	Sco	26	19
Johnny Graham	HB	Sco	26	0
Jack Gordon	FW	Sco	25	11
Jimmy Ross	FW	Sco	26	21
John Goodall	FW	Eng	26	22
Fred Dewhurst	FW	Eng	21	13
Sam Thompson	FW	Sco	21	6
Robert Mills-Roberts	GK	Wal	7	0
Richard Whittle	FB	Eng	1	1
George Drummond	HB	Sco	16	1
Willie Graham	HB	Sco	5	0
Jack Edwards	FW	Eng	4	3
Archie Goodall	FW	Ire	2	1
Jock Inglis	FW	Eng	1	1

Chairman / Manager: Billy Sudell

*Goalkeeper James Trainer and half-back Sandy Robertson played in the majority of the season's league fixtures, but were replaced for the FA Cup final by Robert Mills-Roberts and George Drummond respectively. Trainer was not qualified to play in the FA Cup. Preston North End legend Nick Ross wasn't a part of the Invincibles squad. He spent this single season at Everton, returning to Preston for the 1889-90 league win.

NICK AND JIMMY ROSS

Nicholas John Ross (known as 'Nick', but sometimes referred to as 'Jack') was described by journalist Jimmy Catton as 'the most brilliant back of his day, if not of all time'. Captain and lynchpin of Preston North End, he actually missed the side's double win as he spent season 1888-89 at Everton, on wages of £10 per month. Catton described a formidable opponent: 'His teeth were discoloured, almost green near the gums, and he hissed through them as he played. He was the demon back, the best I ever saw.' Health problems curtailed Nick's career, and he died of tuberculosis in 1894, aged just 31. Younger brother Jimmy Ross did play in Preston's 'Invincibles' team, and scored 18 goals over the season. Overall, Jimmy scored 250 goals in 220 games for Preston. He also played for Liverpool, Burnley, and Manchester City, and played a key role in the formation of the Association Footballers' Union.

Preston North End, 1888
(Back: Billy Sudell, Bob Holmes, Nick Ross, David Russell, Bob Howarth, Johnny Graham, Robert Mills-Roberts; Front: Jack Gordon, Jimmy Ross, John Goodall, Fred Dewhurst, Geordie Drummond)

PENALTY!

The penalty kick was introduced to football in 1891, and was the brainchild of Irishman William McCrum. A goalkeeper for Mitford FC and a member of the Irish FA, McCrum proposed the penalty as a solution to reduce the number of deliberate fouls being committed to prevent a goal. The idea was submitted to the IFAB – and initially rejected. However, following a high-profile incident during an FA Cup quarter-final in which a Notts County defender prevented Stoke City from scoring via a blatant goal-line handball, the penalty was incorporated into the Laws of the Game. Initially there was no penalty area or penalty spot, so the original penalty kick was somewhat different to the modern version. The kick could be taken from any point 12 yards from the goal-line, and the goalkeeper could advance six yards off his line, allowing keepers to narrow the angle. The introduction of the penalty brought derision from amateur players, who detested the implication that any player would commit a deliberate or 'professional' foul. Great Corinthian CB Cry wrote, 'It is a standing insult to sportsmen to have to play under a rule which assumes that the players intend to trip, hack and push their opponents, and behave like cads of the most unscrupulous kidney.' The first penalty was awarded on 14 September 1891 to Wolverhampton Wanderers against Accrington FC. Joseph 'Billy' Heath took the kick – and scored in a 5-0 win.

From the IFAB minute book, 2 June 1891: 'If any player shall intentionally trip or hold an opposing player, or deliberately handle the ball, within 12 yards from his own goal-line, the referee shall, on appeal, award the opposing side a penalty kick, to be taken from any point 12 yards from the goal-line, under the following conditions: All players, with the exception of the goalkeeper (who shall not advance more than six yards from the goal-line) shall stand at least six yards behind the ball. The ball shall be in play when the kick is taken, and a goal may be scored from the penalty kick.'

SHEFFIELD UNITED

Sheffield United FC was formed in 1889 to generate income at the Bramall Lane ground, which had recently been vacated by the Wednesday. A Sheffield United Cricket Club had played at Bramall Lane since 1855. The key instigator in the formation of the football club was Charles Clegg, an inexorable figure in Sheffield sports, who was president of the cricket club, president of the Sheffield FA, and president of the Wednesday – and would go on to become president of the FA. The formation of the new club was controversial, and shrouded in secrecy. It was revealed in a local paper that United were arranging practice matches to trial new players, including several from Scotland. Igniting a famous rivalry, Wednesday pointed out that they relied on local talent, and would leave the 'foreign alternative' to the newcomers. Not all of United's 'foreign' players made the grade. 'The local men in the new team all showed fair form,' said the *Sheffield and Rotherham Independent*, 'but one or two of the Scotchmen looked rather off colour.' The latter were eventually 'sent upon a return journey across the Tweed'. Among the 'local men' were goalkeeper Charlie Howlett, who had notoriously bad eyesight, and once conceded 13 goals in an FA Cup tie against Bolton, and the club's first goalscorer Billy Mosforth, the famous England international winger who had previously been the first goalscorer for Wednesday. The club initially played in white shirts, but switched to red and white stripes in 1890. Early seasons were spent in the Midland Counties League and then the Northern League before United were admitted to the newly-expanded Football League's second division in 1892. The club won promotion in its first season, and quickly established itself as a leading first division side. United's star player at that time was left-half Ernest 'Nudger' Needham, who would make more than 460 appearances for the club. Needham became captain, and led United to a Football League championship win in 1897-98. The club has never won the league since.

CUP PRIORITY

When Blackburn Rovers arrived at the Oval in March 1892 for the club's sixth FA Cup final, hopes of a fifth win seemed slim. Their opponents were Notts County, who had thrashed Rovers 7-1 in a league fixture just seven days earlier. 'How the mighty are fallen!' said the *Blackburn Standard*. Newspaper pundits saw only one winner. 'The result of the league match between these clubs on Saturday would point to Notts as being winners of the cup,' predicted the *Pall Mall Gazette*. However, in the words of Jimmy Catton, 'Rovers did not distress themselves that day.' They were saving themselves for the cup. At least 23,000 spectators watched the final, making it the highest-attended club football match there had ever been. Rovers had written to the Lancashire and Yorkshire Railway Company requesting that the usual fare to London be reduced for supporters travelling to the cup final. The request was refused, and the fare remained at 10s. Nevertheless, many fans made the journey. 'It speedily became apparent that each club had a large following of partisans present,' reported *Lloyd's Weekly*, 'and not only did the Lancashire lads and the Nottingham "lambs" put themselves "in evidence" by the energetic way they urged on their respective favourites, but not a few of them wore in their headgear a card, on which was printed, "Play up Rovers!" or "Play up Notts!"' Rovers attacked County with a fast and effective passing game, and raced to a 3-0 half-time lead with goals from Geordie Dewar, Jack Southworth and William Townley. In the second half, Rovers were content to sit back and defend. County pulled a goal back, but it wasn't enough. In winning their fifth FA Cup final, Rovers equalled the record of Wanderers. 'Without doing any injustice to the renowned amateur club of 15 years ago,' said the *Daily News*, 'it may fairly be said, taking into consideration the enormous development of skill within the last few seasons, that the Rovers have accomplished the biggest performance in the history of English association football.'

The goal net was invented by Everton fan and civil engineer John Alexander Brodie. He was prompted into action by a wrongly-disallowed goal that robbed his team of a victory against Accrington in 1889. Before goal nets, it was often difficult for officials to tell whether the ball had gone inside or outside the posts. This wasn't made any easier by the fact that spectators would stand along the goal-line, and would sometimes – whether accidentally or on purpose – prevent goals. Brodie realised that a net could confirm whether or not a goal had been scored, and also keep spectators off the line. He trialled his invention on Stanley Park, and filed a patent in 1890. In January 1891, Brodie persuaded the FA to trial his nets during a North versus South match at Nottingham Forest's Town Ground. Coincidentally for Brodie, it was an Everton player, the great Fred Geary, who scored the first goal of the match, and therefore became the first footballer to hit the back of the net. Another Everton forward, Edgar Chadwick, also scored in a 3-0 win for the North. 'The goal nets introduced by a Liverpool man were used and were considered by the goalkeeper a very useful introduction,' reported the *Yorkshire Herald*. The *Birmingham Daily Post*, however, thought the trial inconclusive: 'There was no question about any of the goals scored, and the efficacy of the nets could not be judged.' Nevertheless, at a meeting of the Football League in September 1891 it was resolved that 'Brodie's goal nets should be used in all league matches'. The *Birmingham Daily Post* soon embraced nets after they helped Aston Villa claim a 5-1 win over Notts County. 'The goal nets were a great service,' the paper commented, 'as two of the points scored by the Villa were from shots just under the bar, and from a distance it was difficult to tell whether the ball had gone through. Finding the ball inside the net, however, does away with doubt, and the referee is prevented from giving a questionable decision.' Brodie later worked as chief engineer on the Mersey Tunnel, but said the goal net was his finest achievement.

SPANISH SEVILLA

Spain's first football club was Sevilla, which was formed by British residents of Seville in 1890, 'after a deal of talk and a limited consumption of small beer'. The club initially arranged matches between its members ('about half and half Spanish and British') on Sunday mornings until getting out of bed became a problem. Unlike those in Britain, Spanish footballers were not guaranteed a half-holiday on a Saturday afternoon. However, as Sevilla's membership was mostly drawn from a few local manufacturing businesses, players were able to negotiate Saturday afternoons off for football. Desperately seeking opposition, Sevilla wrote to the Huelva Recreation Club and requested that they raise a football team. Huelva had been formed by a pair of Scottish doctors working at the Rio Tinto mines in the previous year, but the club hadn't yet tried association football. Nevertheless, the challenge was accepted, and the first football match on Spanish soil took place at the Tablada Racecourse on 8 March 1890, in a heavy downpour of rain. 'The players presented a motley appearance, all kinds of costumes being in requisition,' reported a Sevilla club member. 'Our left wing, never before having the honour of belonging to any athletic club, appeared on the scene in night dress, in the shape of a fantastically patterned suit of pyjamas.' The hardy gaggle of around 140 spectators found great amusement in his outfit: 'He was hailed with shouts of derisive laughter, and dubbed by the natives as Clown Yugles.' Sevilla won the match 2-0, with the first goal scored by Ritson, and the second by pyjama man Yugles ('unexpectedly by all, not less so by himself'). A slap-up meal followed. 'This being the first known football contest in the south of Spain, probably all of Spain, it was thought worthy of a special banquet,' said the Sevilla member. Sevilla is directly linked to the current Sevilla FC, which was officially founded in 1902. The English-style 'FC' indicates that the club was founded by British expats. Huelva Recreation Club is now known as Recreativo de Huelva.

EVERTON

St Domingo's FC was formed in 1878 by a minister at the St Domingo Methodist Church in the Everton district of Liverpool. The club changed its name to Everton FC during a meeting at the Queen's Head Hotel in the following November. Everton initially played on Stanley Park, for a time in black jerseys with a crimson sash, leading to early nickname 'the Black Watch'. (The club didn't adopt blue shirts until 1901.) In 1884, the club moved to a new ground, named Anfield. The club's growing popularity led to rapid development of the ground, which became one of the biggest and best in the country. Everton were founder members of the Football League, and they won the league in 1890-91, pipping Preston North End to the title by two points. Fred Geary scored 21 goals that season, forming a fearsome attacking trio with Edgar Chadwick and Alf Milward. Scottish full-back Dan Doyle was the club's title-winning captain. A dispute over ownership and rent saw Everton leave Anfield in 1892. The club crossed Stanley Park and built a new home – Goodison Park.

Everton, 1892
(Geary front centre, Chadwick and Milward front right)

133

ATTENDANCE EVOLUTION

Season	FA Cup Final	Top League Match*
1872-73	2,000	-
1873-74	3,000	-
1874-75	2,000	-
1875-76	3,500	-
1876-77	3,000	-
1877-78	4,500	-
1878-79	5,000	-
1879-80	6,000	-
1880-81	4,000	-
1881-82	6,500	-
1882-83	8,000	-
1883-84	4,000	-
1884-85	12,500	-
1885-86	15,000	-
1886-87	15,500	-
1887-88	19,000	-
1888-89	22,000	7,500
1889-90	20,000	10,000
1890-91	23,000	11,000
1891-92	32,800	10,000
1892-93	45,000	13,000
1893-94	37,000	14,000
1894-95	42,500	16,000
1895-96	48,800	16,000
1896-97	65,800	16,000
1897-98	62,000	17,500
1898-99	73,800	20,500
1899-1900	68,945	20,000

*Match between two top-supported Football League sides.

TOP TOFFEES

Everton were the top-supported Football League side of the Victorian era. For the first four league seasons, Everton played at Anfield, where they attracted average attendances of around 10,000. They were league champions in 1890-91, with the great Fred Geary the crowd's goalscoring favourite. The move to Goodison Park in 1892 boosted average attendances to around 13,000, and within another five years they were up to around 17,500. Everton had the highest average attendance of any club during the first 10 league seasons, only being surpassed towards the end of the era by Aston Villa, Newcastle United and Manchester City. Aston Villa had the highest average attendance of the 1899-1900 season of around 20,000. The great occasion of the FA Cup final drew substantially higher crowds than top league matches. Final attendances rose from 2,000 in 1873 to almost 69,000 in 1900.

AGGRESSIVE ANTAGONISTS

The 1889 Cheshire Cup final between Crewe Alexandra and Northwich Victoria was overshadowed by post-match violence. Northwich won the final 3-1, but things really kicked off afterwards at Middlewich Station. 'Both teams had assembled on opposite platforms waiting for trains,' reported the *Illustrated Police News*, 'and whilst there they began hooting and cheering, and then one man challenged an aggressive antagonist to fight. Both leaped onto the metals and fought desperately 'til separated by some railway officials. Then a number of Northwich men ran across the line and stormed the platform occupied by the Crewe men, the uninterested passengers bolting right and left while the fight proceeded.' By the time the police arrived, Northwich had 'gained possession' of the Crewe platform. The fight now over, the Crewe players were escorted by police to their train, 'many of them carrying marks that will distinguish them for some time'.

LIVERPOOL

Liverpool FC was founded by former Everton club president John Houlding in 1892. Everton played at Anfield at that time, and Houlding was their landlord. A dispute arose between Everton and Houlding regarding rent and ownership of the ground. As a result, Everton decided to move to Goodison Park, leaving Houlding with an empty Anfield. His response was to form a new club – also called Everton FC. Houlding even approached the Football League requesting to take over the original Everton's fixtures and league position. The request was refused, and Houlding was also told to change his club's name. He did so – and the club became Liverpool FC. So Houlding had a ground and a name, but he didn't have a team. He turned to his friend 'Honest' John McKenna, an Irish businessman who effectively became Liverpool's first manager. McKenna used his connections in Scotland to sign 13 Scottish players, including Duncan McLean, James McBride and Malcolm McVean. Known as the 'team of Macs', Liverpool was the first English club to field an entire side of non-English players. The club won its first-ever match 7-1 against Rotherham Town. Within a year, the club had won the Liverpool Senior Cup, defeating Everton 1-0 in the final – although the amateur match isn't considered an 'official' Merseyside derby. After a season in the Lancashire League, in 1893 Liverpool were elected to the Football League second division, alongside fellow newcomers Newcastle United and Woolwich Arsenal. Liverpool topped the division in their first season, and beat Newton Heath 2-0 in a test match play-off to secure promotion to the first division. The club had now reached the same tier as Everton, and the first 'official' Merseyside derby was played at Goodison Park on 13 October 1894. Everton won 3-0, and it wouldn't be until 1897-98 that Liverpool finally registered a league win over their rivals. It was the arrival of manager Tom Watson in 1896 that really propelled Liverpool towards greatness. The club would win the league twice during the Edwardian era under Watson's leadership.

JOHN GOODALL

Born in 1863, John Goodall was labelled 'the first Scotsman who ever played for England'. Although raised by Scottish parents in Kilmarnock, he was born in London, and won 14 caps for England, scoring 12 goals. (His brother Archie was born in Ireland, and won 10 caps for his birth country.) Jimmy Catton wrote that Goodall was 'quiet as an old sheep, but such a player'. A great goalscorer – he scored 50 goals in 56 games for Preston North End – Goodall was also an unselfish goal creator. 'We never bothered about who got the goals,' he said. 'They belonged to the side, not the man.' Having starred as one of Preston's double-winning 'Invincibles', Goodall moved to Derby County, where he played alongside and mentored Steve Bloomer. Remarkably, Goodall played football until he was 50 years old, acting as player-manager of Watford, and playing in France with RC Roubaix, before seeing out his long career at Mardy AFC in Wales. Away from football, he kept pet foxes, and ran a bird shop. Goodall died in Watford in 1942.

Playing in a layer of snow that made passing impossible, the men of Preston North End and Notts County were 'chilled to the bone' during this league match at Deepdale in December 1891. However, as the *North Eastern Daily Gazette* observed, feeling the cold was no excuse for what happened next in a 'by no means pleasant' game that produced 'some remarkable scenes'. Preston were no longer the Invincibles, but were still one of the top teams in the country, and they managed to take the lead via a Jimmy Ross free-kick. There was then 'a collision' between Preston's Geordie Drummond and Notts's Jimmy Oswald, with the latter accusing the former of deliberately kicking him 'in the most dangerous part of the body'. The pair exchanged blows, and were ordered off the field by referee Mr Lockett. However, within a few minutes, Drummond returned to the field – and promptly scored two goals to give Preston a 3-0 half-time lead. When Drummond made it 4-0 after the break, a Notts official stormed onto the pitch and ordered his men back to the pavilion. Half of the team obliged, leaving only five Notts players (Harry Daft, David Calderhead, Tom McLean, John Hendry, and goalkeeper George Toone) to face the 11 Prestonians. The outnumbered men appealed to the referee to end the game, if not for the discrepancy in numbers then due to the terrible weather and failing light. But Mr Lockett refused, and the five were forced to play out the remainder of the match. Sadly, this is not a story of a remarkable comeback. The remaining members of the Notts team 'stuck to their work splendidly', and repeatedly caught the marauding Preston forwards offside. Busied keeper Toone was specifically singled out for praise. However, their best efforts were in vain. Drummond scored another goal, as did Ross, to give Preston a 6-0 win in the strangest of circumstances. Edinburgh-born Drummond – the hero or villain of this story, depending on your viewpoint – played almost 140 games for Preston, winning the league and cup, and went on to become the club's trainer.

On the very same day in December 1891 that half of the Notts County team walked off the field at Preston, the entire Blackburn Rovers team – with the notable exception of goalkeeper Herby Arthur – left the field at Burnley. The match was played in dreadful conditions, with high winds driving a snowstorm. Burnley, playing with the wind at their backs, were able to take advantage, scoring three times within the first 35 minutes. After the third goal went between his posts, former England international Arthur attempted to trick the referee into thinking the shot had gone wide. But the ref was the formidable Charles Clegg, and he wasn't to be trifled with. Burnley led 3-0 at half-time. With the weather showing no sign of abating, Blackburn were reluctant to play the second half, and offered to concede the match. Burnley refused. Several Blackburn players were still sheltering in the pavilion when Clegg restarted the match. They were soon joined by Alex Stewart of Burnley and Joe Lofthouse of Blackburn, who were sent off by referee Clegg after exchanging blows. What happened next was extraordinary – and is one of the most famous incidents in Victorian football. The remaining Blackburn players, except for Arthur, followed Lofthouse from the field 'amid derisive cheers'. That left Blackburn's lone goalkeeper Arthur facing 10 men of Burnley. Clegg showed no mercy, and ordered that the game should continue. Burnley immediately charged up the field towards the Blackburn goal. Arthur initially pursued them, but then he had a realisation and stopped. Tom Nicol rolled the ball into the empty Blackburn goal, and Arthur immediately yelled, 'Offside!' The crowd burst into laughter, and Clegg conceded that Arthur's call was correct, awarding him a free-kick. A fed-up Arthur booted the ball into his own goal, and Clegg finally gave up, abandoning the game with 30 minutes left to play. The FA subsequently banned Lofthouse and Stewart, and resolved that in future any player leaving the field without the consent of the referee would be guilty of gross misconduct.

A LEAGUE OF THEIR OWN

The Scottish Football League kicked off in the 1890-91 season with 11 participants – until Renton were expelled for professionalism, which was still outlawed in Scotland. 'Nothing like it has been known in the history of the game,' said one newspaper of the affair that saw one of Scottish football's biggest names banned for playing a match against the blacklisted St Bernard's club. Many of Renton's players headed across the border to play, professionally, for English clubs. (Renton were reinstated in the following season following a protest.) In fact, professionalism was rife throughout Scottish football, with many clubs making illicit payments to 'veiled' pros. A notable exception was the fiercely amateur Queen's Park, which refused to even attend the first meeting of the league, concerned that its formation would be detrimental to amateur clubs. Instead, Queen's Park preferred to continue to arrange friendly matches against high-profile English and Scottish clubs. That left the likes of Celtic, Rangers, and Hearts competing in the league with less well-known (and now defunct) sides such as Cowlairs, Cambuslang, and Abercorn. There were further quandaries ahead. Jack Bell of Dumbarton scored 20 goals in just 18 matches to fire his club to the top of the table. However, although Dumbarton had a superior goal difference, the club finished level on points with Rangers. Goal difference didn't count, so a play-off match was arranged. 8,000 spectators attended at Cathkin Park in Glasgow, where Rangers took a 2-0 half-time lead, only for Dumbarton to fight back to 2-2. The match ended as a draw, and it was decided that the league title would be shared – the only time in history that has happened. (Dumbarton won the league outright in the following season, with Bell again the top scorer.) At the other end of the league table, Cowlairs finished bottom after having points deducted for fielding ineligible players. The club was deselected from the league, and never returned to the Scottish top flight, eventually being boarded up like an old abandoned mine in 1896.

SCOTTISH LEAGUE WINNERS

Season	Winner	Runner-up
1890–91	Dumbarton and Rangers	n/a
1891–92	Dumbarton	Celtic
1892–93	Celtic	Rangers
1893–94	Celtic	Heart of Midlothian
1894–95	Heart of Midlothian	Celtic
1895–96	Celtic	Rangers
1896–97	Heart of Midlothian	Hibernian
1897–98	Celtic	Rangers
1898–99	Rangers	Heart of Midlothian
1899–1900	Rangers	Celtic

SCOTTISH LEAGUE TOP GOALSCORERS

Season	Player (Club)	
1890–91	Jack Bell (Dumbarton)	20
1891–92	Jack Bell (Dumbarton)	23
1892–93	Sandy McMahon (Celtic)	11
	John Campbell II (Celtic)	11
1893–94	Sandy McMahon (Celtic)	16
1894–95	James Miller (Clyde)	12
1895–96	Allan Martin (Celtic)	19
1896–97	Willie Taylor (Heart of Midlothian)	12
1897–98	Robert Hamilton (Rangers)	18
1898–99	Robert Hamilton (Rangers)	25
1899–1900	Robert Hamilton (Rangers)	15
	William Michael (Hearts)	15

SUNDERLAND

One of the most successful Football League sides of the Victorian era, Sunderland AFC began life in 1879 as the Sunderland and District Teachers' Association Football Club. Formed at the Hendon Board School by headteacher James Allan, the club initially played its matches at the nearby Blue House Field – and played in blue jerseys. Sunderland's first recorded match was on 13 November 1880 against Ferryhill, and resulted in a 1-0 defeat. The club opened its doors to non-teachers in 1881, when it adopted its current name. The catalyst for Sunderland's success was the advent of professionalism. The club was one of the first in England to recruit Scottish professionals, and gradually built up an impressive squad, including the likes of prolific centre-forward John Campbell, goalkeeper Ted Doig, and centre-back John Auld. Club founder James Allan, disillusioned by the growth of professionalism, quit in 1888 to form Sunderland Albion, creating a bitter, if short-lived, rivalry. By now, Sunderland were playing in red and white stripes, at the Newcastle Road Ground, and were managed by the great Tom Watson. The club was elected to the Football League in 1890, having promised to pay travelling expenses to opponents making the trip to the North East. Driven by Campbell's goals, the 'team of all talents' won the league three times in its first five attempts.

DRESSING ROOM CHAT

In an 1889 column entitled 'Dressing Room Chat', the *Northern Echo* revealed the latest behind-the-scenes gossip from Sunderland. The club's new signing, John Auld, had been installed as the manager of an 'extensive' boot and shoe shop opposite Sunderland Railway Station. However, he was unlikely to frequent any of the town's pubs. 'Six members of the Sunderland team, including Auld, are teetotallers,' revealed the paper, 'and there are seven non-smokers.'

FOOTBALL MANAGER

Often referred to as the first great football manager, Tom Watson was highly influential in the early development of three of England's biggest clubs. Born in Newcastle in 1859, Watson was involved with several local sides, and was secretary of Newcastle's West End, and then East End – the club that became Newcastle United. As secretary, it was Watson's job to arrange fixtures, keep records, and submit match details to local papers. At the time, there was no such thing as a football manager. But Watson went beyond the remit of secretary, and got involved in team selection, tactics and player recruitment – becoming a football manger in all but name. Watson pioneered the recruitment of players from Scotland, offering star players from north of the border lucrative professional contracts. He would travel to Scotland on scouting missions at great personal risk, amid tales of English player-poachers being trussed up and ducked in barrels of water by angry Scottish football folk. At East End, Watson tempted players with the offer of a £5 signing-on fee and a job in a Newcastle factory. He oversaw East End's entry into competitive football, via the FA Cup and the Northern League. Then, in 1889, Watson was poached by Sunderland after being approached in a Newcastle pub and offered £100 a year and a new suit. In truth, it was probably Sunderland's transfer power that attracted Watson. Super-rich Sunderland could afford to pay high wages and 'special retainers', meaning Watson could recruit the very best Scottish players, such as John Campbell from Renton and John Auld from Third Lanark. Watson's cross-border raids enabled him to build Sunderland's 'team of all talents', which won three league titles under his stewardship. He remains the most successful manager in Sunderland's history. Renowned for his success on and off the field, Watson was head-hunted by Liverpool in 1896. He won two league titles with Liverpool at the beginning of the 20th century, becoming the first manager to win the league with two different clubs.

ENGLAND CAPTAINS

The 24 men who captained England during the Victorian era:

Name	From	Matches
Cuthbert Ottaway	1872	2
Alexander Morten	1873	1
CW Alcock	1875	1
Hubert Heron	1876	1
William Rawson	1877	1
Arthur Cursham	1878	2*
Henry Wace	1879	1*
Charles Wollaston	1880	1
Francis Sparks	1880	1
Jack Hunter	1881	1
Norman Bailey	1881	15
Charles Bambridge	1882	2
John Hudson	1883	1
Percy Walters	1886	5
Tinsley Lindley	1888	4
John Brodie	1889	1
John Goodall	1891	2
Billy Moon	1891	1
Arthur Tempest Blackiston Dunn	1892	2
George Cotterill	1893	2
Robert Holmes	1894	3
Charles Wreford-Brown	1895	3**
Robert Cunliffe Gosling	1895	1**
Gilbert Smith	1896	13

*Cursham is thought to have captained England versus Wales in 1879, although some sources state it was Wace.
**Wreford-Brown is thought to have captained England versus Wales in 1894, although some sources state it was Gosling.

GO SMITH

Gilbert Oswald Smith, known as GO (or Jo), was arguably the greatest amateur footballer of the Victorian era. Born in 1869, he was educated at Charterhouse and Oxford, and became a school teacher. He played football primarily for the Corinthians, but also for Old Carthusians and the Casuals. Smith captained the Corinthians, and scored 132 goals in 137 games for England's most prominent amateur club. Smith didn't look much like a footballer. 'He struck me as rather frail in physique,' wrote Jimmy Catton, 'On the field he was courageous and most unselfish. In his case, mind triumphed over muscle by quickness of decision, the swiftness of his movements, the perfect simplicity of his style, the swerve and balance of his body, and his neatness of footwork.' Smith became England captain in 1896, and played 20 times for his country, scoring 11 goals. Unlike some leading amateurs, Smith enjoyed mutual respect with professionals. England teammate Steve Bloomer called Smith 'the finest type of amateur', and the finest forward he ever saw or played with.

FOREIGN INVASION

An 1892 survey of the nationality of Football League players in England found that the majority of them were 'foreigners'. Out of 176 players from 16 clubs, 99 were from Scotland, 73 from England, three from Wales, and one from Ireland. 'The Sunderland team were Scotch to a man,' reported the survey, 'and the representatives of Preston North End, Everton, and Notts included respectively eight, seven, and eight players from over the border. In these circumstances it is rather hard to see where local patriotism comes in.' The survey report ended with a rather weak joke: 'Everton being the home of toffee manufacture, it is suggested that their football team should, in future, be known as the Butter Scotchmen.'

DIAMOND REFEREE

Football referee William Eddison sued the *London Evening News* in 1893 after the paper wrongly accused him of being a diamond thief. The paper said the Bradford ref had travelled to the US, where he had stolen $1,200 worth of diamonds from a company in New York, then borrowed a large amount of money from friends in Connecticut, before disappearing. Eddison was awarded £50 in damages and an apology.

TIGHT BOOTS

In 1892, footballer Thomas Hewitt died while changing his boots. The 33-year-old, who worked as a scavenger, was playing for Ashton Town at the Ashton Athletic Grounds in Greater Manchester. 'When five minutes had elapsed he went to change boots with a spectator, the boots he was then wearing pinching him,' reported the *North Eastern Daily Gazette*. 'While sitting on the ground lacing the boots he fell backwards, and died before he could be carried into the pavilion.'

GAME OF THREE HALVES

Sunderland and Derby County played a complicated game of three halves at Sunderland's Newcastle Road ground in September 1894. The weather was perfect, and 8,000 spectators turned up, but, unfortunately, the referee didn't. Tom Kirkham had missed his train connection, so a chap named John Conqueror volunteered to take his place. The match kicked off, the great John Campbell scored for Sunderland, and by half-time the 'team of all talents' held a 3-0 lead. Then Mr Kirkham arrived, declared the first 45 minutes null and void, and ordered the match to be restarted under his stewardship. Sunderland's three goals were erased from the records, and the second half became the first half. If it seemed like the referee had done Derby a favour, that didn't prove to be the case. Perhaps mindful that a first half score had already been telegraphed to newspapers around the country, Sunderland managed to exactly reproduce it in the second first half, playing 'strongly and finely', and restoring their 3-0 lead. Then came the third half, which was actually, of course, the first second half. By this time, despite the best efforts of goalkeeper John Robinson, Derby were resigned to a hiding. John Campbell scored again, and Sunderland blitzed the third half 5-0. They'd scored 11 goals over the three halves, but only the second and third halves counted, so the official final score was 8-0 to Sunderland. Goalkeeper Robinson blamed the huge defeat not on the referee but on his failure to find any rice pudding in Sunderland before the match. Robinson, whose motto was 'no pudding, no points', ate a bowl of rice pudding before every match. Dessert-based superstition aside, Derby had been subjected to an unusually extended thrashing. The result, despite its strange circumstances, highlighted the huge gulf in class between the two sides. Sunderland went on to win the league, while Derby finished second bottom, avoiding relegation courtesy only of a narrow test match win over Notts County.

THE CRYSTAL PALACE

After football was banned at the Oval, the FA Cup final found a new permanent home at the Crystal Palace. Every final between 1895 and 1914 was played at the new venue. The Crystal Palace itself was a huge plate-glass building originally erected in London's Hyde Park for the 1851 Great Exhibition. It was subsequently relocated to Sydenham Hill in South London, with the surrounding area becoming known as Crystal Palace. (The building itself burnt down in 1936.) The building was set in landscaped grounds with ornamental gardens and water features, which proved a popular attraction. However, by 1895 visitor numbers were falling, and it was decided to open the grounds to football. It provided a substantially bigger space than the Oval. Around 32,000 watched the last FA Cup final at the Oval, while more than 42,000 watched the first at the Crystal Palace. That number would swell to almost 69,000 by the end of the Victorian era. 'The great charm of the Crystal Palace was that it was so utterly unlike any other place where football was ordinarily played,' wrote Jimmy Catton. 'The sports arena at the Palace was not a building. It was just a space – sylvan, verdant, luscious – God's work, relatively unspoiled by the designing hands of engineers, architects, and workmen.' The green and pleasant arena was bordered by trees, and overlooked by an old switchback railway rollercoaster ride. The first final at the Palace saw Aston Villa beat West Bromwich Albion 1-0. Villa captain John Devey scored the only goal within 40 seconds of the kick-off, before many spectators had taken their seats. Devey was later involved in a bloody clash of heads with West Brom half-back Tom Higgins. The latter 'had his scalp severely opened', and required stitches and bandages, but returned to finish the match. Famous businessman Colonel John North was so impressed with Higgins' bravery that he sought him out after the game and presented the player with a five pound note. But it was Villa's Devey who was presented with the FA Cup after the first final at football's fine new venue.

FA Cup final at the Crystal Palace, the Graphic, 1895
Aston Villa vs West Bromwich Albion
(Villa's Devey, left, and West Brom's Higgins clash heads)

FA CUP FINALS

Season	Winner	Score	Runner-up
1871–72	Wanderers	1–0	Royal Engineers
1872–73	Wanderers	2–0	Oxford University
1873–74	Oxford University	2–0	Royal Engineers
1874–75	Royal Engineers	1–1 AET	Old Etonians
Replay	Royal Engineers	2–0	Old Etonians
1875–76	Wanderers	1–1 AET	Old Etonians
Replay	Wanderers	3–0	Old Etonians
1876–77	Wanderers	2–1 AET	Oxford University
1877–78	Wanderers	3–1	Royal Engineers
1878–79	Old Etonians	1–0	Clapham Rovers
1879–80	Clapham Rovers	1–0	Oxford University
1880–81	Old Carthusians	3–0	Old Etonians
1881–82	Old Etonians	1–0	Blackburn Rovers
1882–83	Blackburn Olympic	2–1 AET	Old Etonians
1883–84	Blackburn Rovers	2–1	Queen's Park
1884–85	Blackburn Rovers	2–0	Queen's Park
1885–86	Blackburn Rovers	0–0	West Brom
Replay	Blackburn Rovers	2–0	West Brom
1886–87	Aston Villa	2–0	West Brom
1887–88	West Brom	2–1	Preston North End
1888–89	Preston North End	3–0	Wolves
1889–90	Blackburn Rovers	6–1	The Wednesday
1890–91	Blackburn Rovers	3–1	Notts County
1891–92	West Brom	3–0	Aston Villa
1892–93	Wolves	1–0	Everton
1893–94	Notts County	4–1	Bolton Wanderers
1894–95	Aston Villa	1–0	West Brom
1895–96	The Wednesday	2–1	Wolves
1896–97	Aston Villa	3–2	Everton
1897–98	Nottingham Forest	3–1	Derby County
1898–99	Sheffield United	4–1	Derby County
1899–1900	Bury	4–0	Southampton

150

MANCHESTER UNITED

The name 'Manchester United' didn't exist in the Victorian era. The club was formed in 1878 as Newton Heath LYR FC by workers at a Lancashire and Yorkshire Railway depot to the east of Manchester city centre. The 'LYR' distinguished the club from Newton Heath Loco, another club formed by railway workers. Early matches were played on a field near the railway depot, and were mostly friendly matches against other works teams. Competitive football arrived in 1884 via the Manchester and District Challenge Cup, and then in 1886 via the FA Cup. However, in their first ever FA Cup tie, after drawing 2-2 with Fleetwood Town over 90 minutes, Newton Heath refused to play extra time and were eliminated. An appeal for reinstatement was refused, and the club withdrew from the next two FA Cup competitions (in a move echoed by Manchester United in 1999-2000). Newton Heath also took umbrage at the Football League after being overlooked for the inaugural season. Instead, the club became founder members of rival league the Combination, which folded before its first season was completed. Newton Heath then co-founded the more successful Football Alliance, which merged with the Football League in 1892. The club was initially elected to the Football League's first division, but in 1894 became – alongside Darwen – the first club to be relegated. By now, Newton Heath had dropped the 'LYR' suffix. Under the leadership of club secretary/manager Alf Albut, the club took up residency at the Bank Street ground in nearby Clayton. Situated next to a chemical plant, the ground was referred to by some visitors as a 'toxic waste dump'. Key players at this time included Scottish forwards Bob Donaldson and Willie Stewart, and long-serving outside-right Alf Farman. Newton Heath started out wearing green and gold halved jerseys, and switched to red and white halved shirts in the late 1880s. After joining the Football League, they went back to green and gold. All-red shirts were yet to come. Newton Heath would become Manchester United in 1902, and move to Old Trafford in 1910.

SHEER BRUTALITY

In 1894, Newton Heath sued the *Birmingham Gazette* for libel after the newspaper accused the team of 'improper play' in a match against West Bromwich Albion. *Gazette* reporter William Jephcott wrote of the match (which Heath won 4-1): 'It was not football – it was sheer brutality. If these are to be the tactics Newton Heath adopt to win their matches, the sooner the Football Association deal severely with them the better it will be for the game in general.' According to Jephcott, the West Brom players were subjected to a series of 'dirty tricks'. They were kicked in the ankles and the head, and Alf 'Jasper' Geddes was forced to leave the field after receiving a kick to the spine that raised 'a lump as big as a duck egg'. Should Heath continue to play in this style, Jephcott said, 'it will perhaps create an extra run of business for the undertakers'. An aggrieved Newton Heath claimed that such accusations could have a negative effect on their gate receipts, and argued that the match had in fact been fairly contested. Several witnesses, including the referee and a local rector, agreed. Even if foul play had taken place, the club said, it was the responsibility of the FA to deal with it, and no business of the *Gazette*. However, the newspaper insisted that the article had been written in good faith, and that it should be entitled to report foul play without fear of legal action. Reporter Jephcott and several West Brom players, including Geddes, defended the accuracy of the account. It was the first case of its kind involving football, and many observers thought it a waste of judicial resources. Newton Heath won the case, but were awarded just one farthing (a quarter of a penny) in damages, and were ordered to pay their own costs. It was a hollow victory for Heath, and the *Gazette* was praised for its defence of the case. 'The *Gazette* has rendered service to the football world, and to newspaper reporters,' commented the *Dart*. 'As a result, it is improbable that any other club will venture to imitate Newton Heath.'

STEVE BLOOMER

Derby County legend Steve Bloomer was born in 1874. He scored four goals on his Derby debut in 1892, and kept on scoring for 12 seasons. Bloomer hit 291 goals for Derby, plus another 61 during a four-year spell at Middlesbrough. He was the Football League's top goalscorer in five separate seasons, including 1896-97, when he scored 31 goals – including five hat-tricks. Also prolific at international level, Bloomer scored 28 goals in just 23 appearances for England. He remains one of England's all-time stop scorers. After retiring from playing in 1914, Bloomer took a coaching position in Germany. War broke out within weeks of his arrival, and he was interned at the Ruhleben detention camp, where he famously organised and played in a popular inter-camp football league. He later coached in the Netherlands and Spain. A bronze bust of Bloomer was erected outside Derby's Pride Park in 2009.

ORIGINAL SHIRT COLOURS

The earliest recorded colours of Victorian-era football clubs.

Arsenal: Garibaldi red.*
Aston Villa: Scarlet and royal blue hoops.
Blackburn Rovers: White with Maltese cross on left breast.**
Celtic: White.
Corinthian FC: White.
Derby County: Amber and chocolate halves with blue sleeves.
Everton: Blue and white stripes.
Forest/Wanderers: Red and white stripes.
Fulham: Red and white halves.
Leicester City: Black with blue diagonal stripe.
Liverpool: Blue and white halves.
Manchester City: Black with Maltese cross on left breast.**
Manchester United: Green and gold halves.
Newcastle United: Blue.
Notts County: Orange and black.
Queen's Park: Blue.
Sheffield FC: Scarlet and white.
Sheffield United: White.
Sheffield Wednesday: Royal blue and white hoops.
Stoke City: Crimson and blue hoops.
Sunderland: Navy blue.
Tottenham Hotspur: Navy blue with letter H on red shield on left breast.
West Bromwich Albion: White with purple diagonal sash.
West Ham United: Harrovian blue.***
Wolverhampton Wanderers: Blue and white stripes.

*Garibaldi red is associated with Italian general Giuseppe Garibaldi and his Redshirts.
**The Maltese cross was originally associated with the Knights of Malta, and by Victorian times had become a popular motif to symbolise courage.
***Club chairman Arnold Hill was a Harrow School old boy.

THREE-MINUTE GAME

League fixtures over the winter of 1894-95 were severely hampered by bad weather, and snowy circumstances set up one of the shortest matches ever recorded. It was late December, and Stoke were at home to Wolverhampton Wanderers. Despite a heavy snowstorm that had kept all but a few hundred hardy spectators away from the ground, the match got under way as planned. However, the conditions proved to be impossible. Referee T Helme abandoned the match after just three minutes. The fixture was rearranged for mid-January, only for another 'great snowstorm' to interfere. Snow was cleared from the pitch, but meltwater lay 'inches deep'. Mr Helme again called off the match, saying that play was 'altogether out of the question'. They might as well have let the result of the three-minute game stand. When the full match eventually took place, in February, it inevitably ended 0-0.

DIED OF COLD

Jimmy Logan was a Scottish international who played for Sunderland and Aston Villa, but he really made his name at Notts County. Logan's goals fired the second division club to the FA Cup final, where he scored a hat-trick in a 3-1 win over Bolton Wanderers. That final would become known as 'Logan's Match'. Unfortunately, his life and career were tragically short. Logan 'died of cold' a month before his 26th birthday, after playing football in the rain. It was May 1896, and he had recently been transferred from Newcastle United to Loughborough. Some reports said Logan became ill following a trip to Manchester to play Newton Heath. Loughborough arrived without their kit, and had to play in street outfits and 'ordinary boots'. After losing 2-0, the Loughborough players travelled home in their wet clothes. Logan's death was announced a few days later: 'He had been ill for about a week, and the cause of death is said to be pneumonia.'

BRITISH LADIES' FOOTBALL CLUB

'There was an astonishing sight in the neighbourhood of the Nightingale Lane Ground, Crouch End, on Saturday afternoon,' reported *the Sketch* in March 1895. 'Crouch End itself rubbed its eyes and pinched its arms. All through the afternoon train-loads of excited people journeyed over from all parts, and the respectable array of carriages, cabs, and other vehicles marked a record in the history of football.' The event was the first public match of the British Ladies' Football Club, which had been formed a few months earlier by Miss Nettie Honeyball. Advertisements attracted around 30 female footballers, who trained twice-weekly under the tutelage of Tottenham Hotspur wing-half Bill Julian. Honeyball explained that she and her teammates had gained their knowledge and love of football 'from frequent on-looking'. But the formation of the club brought disdain and derision. The ladies were prevented from practicing at the Oval, and were mocked in newspapers. Great interest surrounded the players' outfits, at a time when it was unheard of for women to wear trousers, never mind football shorts. However, the club's baggy blouses and long knickerbockers, tall stockings and fishermen's caps were very modest, and left everything to the imagination. The players also wore shin guards and football boots – with high-heels having been deemed impractical. The match saw the club divided into two teams representing North and South London. It would be idle to attempt any description of the play,' said the *Sketch*. 'The first few minutes were sufficient to show that football by women is totally out of the question. A footballer requires speed, judgement, skill, and pluck. Not one of these four qualities was apparent on Saturday.' The players were jeered, and many of the spectators had left by the time the final whistle blew – with North London winning 7-1. Commercially, however, the match had been a huge success – so much so that Honeyball took her team on a lengthy tour that saw them play around 100 exhibition matches over the next two years.

First match of the British Ladies' Football Club, the Graphic, 1895

SIMPLY STUMBLED

Disgruntled spectators at an 1893 match between Doncaster Rovers and Sheffield Strollers took great exception to the decisions of referee William Young. At the final whistle, they chased Young to the dressing room, and attacked him with sticks and stones. One chap, John Morton, was charged with assault. Morton claimed he had simply stumbled into Young, but was found guilty and fined a pound.

SCOTTISH CUP FINALS

Season	Winner	Score	Runner-up
1873–74	Queen's Park	2–0	Clydesdale
1874–75	Queen's Park	3–0	Renton
1875–76	Queen's Park	1–1	3rd Lanark
Replay	Queen's Park	2–0	3rd Lanark
1876–77	Vale of Leven	1–1	Rangers
Replay	Vale of Leven	1–1	Rangers
Replay 2	Vale of Leven	3–2	Rangers
1877–78	Vale of Leven	1–0	3rd Lanark
1878–79	Vale of Leven	1–1	Rangers
Replay	Vale of Leven	n/a*	Rangers
1879–80	Queen's Park	3–0	Thornliebank
1880–81	Queen's Park	2–1**	Dumbarton
Replay	Queen's Park	3–1	Dumbarton
1881–82	Queen's Park	2–2	Dumbarton
Replay	Queen's Park	4–1	Dumbarton
1882–83	Dumbarton	2–2	Vale of Leven
Replay	Dumbarton	2–1	Vale of Leven
1883–84	Queen's Park	n/a‡	Vale of Leven
1884–85	Renton	0–0	Vale of Leven
Replay	Renton	3–1	Vale of Leven
1885–86	Queen's Park	3–1	Renton
1886–87	Hibernian	2–1	Dumbarton
1887–88	Renton	6–1	Cambuslang
1888–89	3rd Lanark	3–0‡‡	Celtic
Replay	3rd Lanark	2–1	Celtic
1889–90	Queen's Park	1–1	Vale of Leven
Replay	Queen's Park	?–1	Vale of Leven
1890–91	Hearts	1–0	Dumbarton
1891–92	Celtic	1–0^	Queen's Park
Replay	Celtic	5–1	Queen's Park
1892–93	Queen's Park	0–1^^	Celtic
Replay	Queen's Park	2–1	Celtic
1893–94	Rangers	3–1	Celtic
1894–95	St Bernard's	2–1	Renton
1895–96	Hearts	3–1	Hibernian
1896–97	Rangers	5–1	Dumbarton
1897–98	Rangers	2–0	Kilmarnock
1898–99	Celtic	2–0	Rangers
1899–1900	Celtic	4–3	Queen's Park

*Rangers refused to replay in protest over disallowed goal in original match. Vale of Leven handed walkover.
**Replayed after Dumbarton protested result of first match.
‡Vale of Leven failed to turn up. Queen's Park win cup.
‡‡Replayed due to poor playing conditions.
^Match replayed after protests from both teams.
^^Original match result declared void due to pitch conditions.

WELSH CUP FINALS

Season	Winner	Score	Runner-up
1877–78	Wrexham	1–0	Druids
1878–79	Newtown WS	1–0	Wrexham
1879–80	Druids	2–1	Ruthin
1880–81	Druids	2–0	Newtown WS
1881–82	Druids	5–0	Northwich Victoria
1882–83	Wrexham	1–0	Druids
1883–84	Oswestry WS	0–0	Druids
Replay	Oswestry WS	1–0	Druids
1884–85	Druids	1–1	Oswestry WS
Replay	Druids	3–1	Oswestry WS
1885–86	Druids	4–0	Newtown
1886–87	Chirk AAA	2–1	Davenham
1887–88	Chirk AAA	5–0	Newtown
1888–89	Bangor	2–1	Northwich Victoria
1889–90	Chirk AAA	1–0	Wrexham
1890–91	Shrewsbury T	5–2	Wrexham
1891–92	Chirk AAA	2–1	Westminster Rovers
1892–93	Wrexham	2–1	Chirk AAA
1893–94	Chirk AAA	2–0	Westminster Rovers
1894–95	Newtown	3–2	Wrexham
1895–96	Bangor	3–0	Wrexham
1896–97	Wrexham	2–0	Newtown
1897–98	Druids	1–1	Wrexham
Replay	Druids	2–1	Wrexham
1898–99	Druids	2–2	Wrexham
Replay	Druids	1–0	Wrexham
1899–1900	Aberystwyth T	3–0	Druids

FOOTBALLERS' WAGES

The wages paid to footballers varied widely. Some early professionals were paid as little as 4s per week, while by the end of the Victorian era star players at top teams could earn up to £10 per week. In the main, footballers were much better paid than general workers. By 1890, leading footballers were earning four times more than general labourers, and more than many skilled workers. Footballers' wages increased at a much faster rate than those of general workers as the popularity of the sport grew. By 1900, footballers earned 10 times more than general labourers. Win bonuses were common, as were additional payments for extra games and expenses. Players were typically paid a reduced wage over the close season. Even after professionalism was legalised, many footballers retained their old jobs, and therefore had two streams of income. However, there were restrictions placed on professional footballers. From 1893, any player registered with a Football League club could not move to another club without the initial club's permission. This became known as the 'retain and transfer' system. The introduction of this rule, plus proposals to introduce a maximum wage cap, moved leading players such as John Cameron of Everton and Jimmy Ross of Preston to form the Association Footballers' Union. The AFU had 250 members, but wasn't recognised by the FA nor the Football League. Despite the AFU's efforts, a maximum wage of £4 per week was introduced in 1901. This table shows average weekly wages for leading footballers and general workers, plus approximate equivalent amounts today.

| | AV WEEKLY WAGE / EQUIV TODAY | |
YEAR	FOOTBALL	GENERAL
1885	£1 / £60	13s / £37
1890	£3 / £170	13s / £37
1895	£5 / £285	13s / £37
1900	£7 / £400	14s / £40
1901 (CAP)	£4 / £230	14s / £40

ROBERT CUNLIFFE GOSLING

England forward Robert Cunliffe Gosling was an Eton old boy from a large and wealthy family. He made five international appearances in the 1890s, scoring two goals, and captaining his country on at least one occasion. Gosling was described by FA secretary Frederick Wall as 'the richest man who ever played football for England'. Not only was he rich, he was handsome, too. His Corinthians club team-mate CB Fry said Gosling was 'the best-looking man of my acquaintance'. Jimmy Catton, meanwhile, described him as 'the most aristocratic man I ever saw', fitting well with the Corinthians' reputation as a 'team of toffs'. Gosling may have been a gentleman, but he developed a tough reputation on the pitch. He was tall and strong, but quick, too, with noted dribbling and shooting skills. Gosling was also a first class cricketer, and away from football he served as a Justice of the Peace. When he died in 1922, Gosling left behind a £700,000 fortune, worth the equivalent of around £15 million today.

GOLD SOVEREIGNS

The relationship between amateurs and professionals, or 'gentlemen' and 'players', was often uncomfortable, particularly on international duty. Some amateurs refused to speak to their professional teammates, and there were tales of separate train carriages and dressing rooms. For the match against Scotland in 1898, England were captained by the Corinthian Charles Wreford-Brown, the man who first called football 'soccer'. After Fred Wheldon scored England's first goal, Wreford-Brown reached into the pocket of his knickerbockers, and handed the Aston Villa forward a gold sovereign. Then Steve Bloomer scored, and Wreford-Brown gave him the same reward. When Bloomer scored his second goal, and England's third, Wreford-Brown gave the Derby hero another gold sovereign and remarked, 'If you keep this up, Steve, I shall have to go for my handbag!' Patronising? Professional footballers were relatively well paid by this time, but Bloomer accepted his golden goal bonus with good grace.

PLAY FOR HIS PAPERS

At a Football League management meeting in late 1898, committee member Charles Sutcliffe read out a controversial letter written by a prominent player to an unnamed club stating that, if the club were interested in engaging him, he would 'play for his papers', or 'so play that his club would be pleased to get rid of him'. In other words, he would deliberately play badly in order to engineer a move. The recently-formed Association Footballers' Union wrote to the league demanding to see the letter in order that the player could be punished. But Sutcliffe said he no longer had the letter in his possession. He subsequently said that the club to whom the letter belonged had declined to produce it, stating that the player concerned had been disciplined internally and was playing for them again, 'all differences having been settled'.

TWO JOHN CAMPBELLS

The football scoring charts of the early 1890s were dominated by two John Campbells – John Campbell of Sunderland, and John Campbell of Aston Villa. Both were Scots, both were known as 'Johnny', both were centre-forwards, and both scored the goals that led their teams to Football League glory. It was Sunderland's John Campbell, born in 1870, who first came to prominence. Campbell had played – and scored – against Sunderland for Renton in a friendly in 1888. In the following season, Sunderland signed three members of the Renton front-line, known as the 'Renton Charge' – centre-forward Campbell, inside-left David Hannah, and outside-right John Harvie. Sunderland were building the 'team of all talents', and Campbell was its focal point. He was the country's top scorer in 1891-92, 1892-93 and 1894-5, firing his club to three league titles. His tally of 32 goals in 1891-92 was the highest of any player in the Victorian era. Campbell scored 133 goals in 186 games for Sunderland, and if his memory has faded in the memory of Sunderland fans that can only be because in 1897 he moved to Newcastle. Aston Villa's John Campbell, born in 1871, was Scottish international and Scottish league and cup champion when he was signed from Celtic in 1895. He was the top scorer in Scotland in 1892-93, when Celtic won the league, and he scored two goals in the 1892 Scottish Cup final, when Celtic beat Queen's Park 5-1. He made an immediate impact in England, scoring 26 goals in 26 games in 1895-96, and topping the goalscoring charts, as Villa won the league. Campbell scored a relatively modest 13 goals in the following season, but he did score in the FA Cup final to secure Villa the league and cup double. He scored the first ever goal at Aston Lower Grounds (the original name for Villa Park), but Campbell's brief but productive time at Villa was coming to an end. He returned to Celtic in 1897, and ended up scoring a total of more than a hundred goals for the Glasgow club, plus five goals for Scotland.

ARSENAL

In 1886, a group of workers from the Dial Square workshop at the Royal Arsenal armaments factory in Woolwich, South London, decided to form a football club. The Dial Square was a turning and engraving workshop named for the sundial over its main entrance. The workshop building still survives today. Dial Square FC's principal founder was a Scotsman called David Danskin. He had played for Kircaldy Wanderers in Fife before moving to London. And Danskin wasn't the only Dial Square worker with football experience. Fred Beardsley had been Nottingham Forest's goalkeeper, but had moved to London after being sacked from his job at a Nottingham armaments factory for taking time off to play football without permission. Danskin organised a whip-round to buy a football, and Beardsley provided a set of 'Garibaldi red' jerseys via his former Forest team-mates. Dial Square's first match was played on 11 December 1886 against a team called Eastern Wanderers on a field at the Isle of Dogs. Dial Square won 6-0. A few weeks later, on Christmas Day 1886, the club changed its name to Royal Arsenal, now representing the whole factory. Royal Arsenal played its initial matches on Plumstead Common, and, after various moves, eventually settled at nearby Manor Field, where they built the Manor Ground. The muddy field had an open sewer running along one side, and no terracing or other facilities. However, the club raised money via a share issue for ground improvements, and remained in Plumstead until 1913. The club turned professional in 1891, and changed its name to Woolwich Arsenal in 1893. However, the club was in serious financial trouble – not least due to the ongoing ground improvement costs – and could not survive on occasional friendly matches and FA Cup ties. An application was made to join the Football League – and was accepted. Woolwich Arsenal were elected to the second division – becoming the first southern club to join the league. Arsenal didn't drop the 'Woolwich' from their name until 1914, after moving to Highbury.

THE LONGEST MATCH

In 1898-99, a league match between the Wednesday and Aston Villa took more than 15 weeks to complete. The first 79 and a half minutes were played on 26 November. Papers reported that the match had 'created a great amount of interest in the cutlery town', and around 20,000 fans were present. The match wasn't completed because it kicked off late. The referee, Aaron Scragg, had missed his train connection and arrived at Wednesday's Olive Grove almost 45 minutes behind schedule. The match eventually got underway, and Wednesday built up a 3-1 lead through Frank Bedingfield, Willie Dryburgh, and Bill Hemingfield. However, after Hemingfield's goal, 'the light hereabouts became very bad'. It was virtually impossible to see the ball, and Mr Scragg abandoned the match with precisely 10 and a half minutes left to play. Quite understandably – considering they were losing – Villa refused to let the result stand, and so the Football League ordered that the balance of the match must be played at a later date. The league also admonished Mr Scragg, advising him that he 'ought to have taken into consideration the state of the railway traffic on Saturdays'. The remainder of the match was played at Olive Grove on 13 March 1899. It was agreed that, after the competitive 10 and a half minutes, the match would be continued as a friendly, with profits going to Wednesday's Harry Davis, who had received a 'paltry' gate from a recent benefit match against Notts County. But, pity for Davis, more than three quarters of those spectators who'd watched the first part of the match didn't bother with its conclusion. Only around 3,000 spectators turned up to watch as, during a 'brief and exciting struggle', Wednesday grabbed a further goal to make the final score 4-1. It had taken 108 days, or three and a half months, to complete the match. The friendly match followed, and Wednesday won that too, triumphing 2-0. However, neither result was representative of the season as a whole. Wednesday were relegated, while Villa won the league.

THE KAFFIRS

In September 1899, a team of black South Africans from the Orange Free State arrived in a steamship at Southampton. They were known as the Kaffir Football Club, and were about to embark on a tour of Britain that would last four months and incorporate almost 50 matches. All this against a back-drop of the newly-erupting second Boer War. The tourists' first match took place at St James' Park, where they lost 6-3 to Newcastle United. 'The Kaffirs had undergone but little pre-liminary training, and they were palpably unfit,' the *Morning Post* reported. Nevertheless, the 'dusky sons of the Orange Free State' were met with a 'cordial reception' from a large crowd. The tone was set for the rest of the tour. 'Kaffir' is, of course, a derogatory term, and the fact that the visitors weren't particularly good at football only lessened the esteem in which they were held. They drew large crowds and were popular with spectators, but were patronised and ridiculed by the press. On one occasion, the Kaffirs played Tottenham Hotspur. 'It was the usual farcical performance, anything but football,' said the London *Standard*, 'the absurdity of the whole thing being emphasised by the Spurs doing without a goalkeeper altogether in the second half.' War broke out between the British and the Boers within weeks of the team's arrival. The Kaffirs publicly supported Britain, and captain Joseph Twayi repeatedly stated his loyalty. 'We Kaffirs have no freedom allowed by the Boers,' he told the *Football News*. 'If the British fight, we fight for them, for we would like our revenge.' The team won praise for donating receipts to a war fund. Despite their apparent lack of talent, the Kaffirs showed no lack of effort during their matches. As the tour progressed, reports began to mention their speed and 'staying power'. Although the Kaffirs never won a game, they did improve. Twayi scored a few goals, and the team's goalkeeper, Adolph, was linked with an approach from an unnamed first division side. Away from the media, the visitors made friends, enter-tained spectators, and raised awareness through football.

WILLIAM 'FATTY' FOULKE

William Foulke was a relative slip of a lad when he first appeared in goal for Sheffield United in 1894. However, his weight grew along with his fame, and he was soon stuck with the nickname 'Fatty'. Over the course of his career, 6ft 2in Foulke ballooned in weight from 13st to as much as 24st. Naturally, Foulke hated the 'Fatty' nickname. Friends called him 'Little Willie', but he was an undeniably big character. He took over the Sheffield United goalkeeping position from Arthur Wharton, and was just as eccentric. Like Wharton, Foulke would sit on and hang from the crossbar during quiet periods of games. Inevitably, as Foulke's weight increased, he snapped a few crossbars. Despite his size, he was incredibly agile, with a 'tremendous smite and prodigious kick'. Foulke won two FA Cup finals and a league championship with Sheffield United. He played for England in 1897, and was for a time referred to as 'the best goalkeeper in the world'. Foulke subsequently played for Chelsea and Bradford City.

In November 1899, the FA organised a short tour of Germany and Austria-Hungary. It was the first time a British national side had travelled to the continent. The tourists were regarded as football missionaries. 'The visit of an English team to Germany may do something to increase the love of the game of football amongst the Kaiser's subjects,' said the *Manchester Times*. FA officials including CW Alcock, Charles Hughes and JJ Bentley travelled with the players, who were a mixture of amateurs and professionals. With the domestic football season in full flow, clubs were reluctant to release their best players. For example, Sheffield United refused to allow Ernest Needham to travel. The tour team's captain was Stanley Briggs of Clapton FC, an amateur who never played for the full England side. However, there were plenty of established internationals, including Jimmy Crabtree of Aston Villa and Fred Forman of Nottingham Forest. The first two matches were played in Berlin on 23 and 24 November. The first game finished 13-2 to the visitors, with Edgar Chadwick, who had recently transferred from Everton to Burnley, scoring six goals. 'The German XI was fairly fast, but the men lacked combination, and were quite outplayed,' reported Reuters. The second game finished 10-2 to the English. Joe Rodgers of Newcastle United scored five of the visitors' goals. Two days later, the action moved to Prague (then part of Austria-Hungary), where the English XI played a German-Austrian XI. This was the best match of the tour. 'The home team played a good game, the defence of their goalkeeper and backs being excellent,' said Reuters. Nevertheless, the English won 8-0. Corinthian Geoffrey Wilson scored a hat-trick. The final game of the tour was played in Karlsruhe, once more against a combined German-Austrian team. The English won 7-0, with Chadwick scoring another hat-trick, bringing the team's overall tally to 38 goals in 4 games. The London *Standard* called the tour 'a decided success', and said the FA had paved the way for more international football in the future.

AMERICAN FOOTBALL

The United States played the round-ball game long before it invented gridiron. Schools and colleges played various kicking games, including the fairly violent 'Boston game', as played by the influential Oneida Football Club, which was formed in 1862. The first game played under association rules on US soil is thought to have taken place just a year after the end of the Civil War, in October 1866 at Waukesha, Wisconsin. According to the *Waukesha Freeman*, it was played 'between the students of Carroll College and the young men of Waukesha'. Despite the fact that the students were outnumbered 22 to 25, they won the match 5-2. (Gridiron football, meanwhile, began to be played and develop during the 1870s.) Association football gradually spread across the US, and found particular popularity in New York, New Jersey, Pennsylvania, and Massachusetts. In 1884, the American Football Association was formed between clubs from those states. The AFA established the American Cup, the nation's first football competition, which was won in its first three seasons by Clark ONT (Our New Thread), a team sponsored by the Clark Thread Company from Newark, New Jersey. Clark was a Scottish company, and there were many British workers at its Newark factory. Harry Holden was the ONT captain, and it was he who was presented with the $200 trophy, which had 'a neat design in silver and gold, with appropriate figures of footballists being engraved on it'. The club was well-supported, with reports of up to 2,000 spectators at its matches. In 1885, ONT organised an unofficial United States versus Canada international match at their Newark ground. Canada won 1-0. A year later, at the same venue, the US won 3-2. Other early American Cup winners included Fall River Rovers of Massachusetts, Pawtucket Free Wanderers of Rhode Island, and Philadelphia Manz of Pennsylvania. Organisational problems and disagreements led to the American Cup being suspended in 1899. The AFA continued to operate until 1925, but never regained its authority. And never a mention of 'soccer'.

MANCHESTER CITY

Formed in 1880 by a pair of church wardens, Manchester City was originally known as West Gorton St Mark's. The club wore black jerseys bearing a Maltese cross – a popular motif of the day. The reference to St Mark's was dropped in 1882, and then the club became plain old Gorton in 1884. In 1887, the club turned professional and moved to Hyde Road, changing its name to Ardwick AFC to better reflect its new location. In 1891, Ardwick joined the Football Alliance, which merged with the Football League in the following season. Financial troubles and a reorganisation led to a final renaming – and, in 1894, Ardwick became Manchester City, adopting new colours of Cambridge blue and white. In that same year, the club signed 19-year-old Welsh winger Billy Meredith, who would go on to become one of the most important players in the club's history. By the end of the Victorian era, Manchester City had won promotion to the first division.

BURY TREASURE

The 1900 FA Cup final – the last of the Victorian era – was contested by two teams that had never previously reached the final. Bury, a mid-table first division side, faced Southern League team Southampton. Neither were in particularly good form. Bury had lost five out of their last six league matches in the run-up to the big game, and Southampton had lost their last four consecutive league matches. It was Bury who prevailed at the Crystal Palace, in front of 69,000 spectators. They had the match won within 25 minutes, with two goals from Jasper McLuckie and one from Willie Wood giving them a 3-0 lead. John Plant scored in the second half to cap a comprehensive 4-0 win. 'When the first telegram arrived at Bury,' *Lloyd's Weekly* reported, 'the utmost enthusiasm prevailed among the enthusiasts awaiting news of the game. Loud cheers were given by the crowds assembled in the streets.'

JOHN CAMERON

Born in Ayr in 1872, John Cameron made his name at Queen's Park, where he became a Scottish international. In 1896, he joined Everton as one of the club's highly-paid professionals. He scored 14 goals in 48 games for Everton, in a truncated stay. Arguments over a wage cap saw Cameron set up the Association Footballers' Union, then quit Everton and the Football League to join Tottenham Hotspur in the Southern League. 'Now look here,' he told a reporter, 'how would any man in business like to have his wages reduced by 25% if his employers could well afford better terms?' Cameron became player-manager of Tottenham in 1899, leading the club to the Southern League title in his first full season in charge, and to FA Cup glory in his second. Cameron also coached in Germany, and, when the war broke out, was interned at Ruhleben alongside the likes of Steve Bloomer. After the war, Cameron became a journalist, writing weekly football columns, and authoring a book, *Association Football and How to Play It*.

ELEPHANT FOOTBALL

In the spring of 1899, the circus came to town. This was Lord John Sanger and Sons' circus ('no connection with George Sanger'), and was billed as 'the largest and grandest show in the world'. A huge convoy of 60 specially-built road cars brought the ringmaster, clowns, tumblers, freaks, 300 horses, lions, exotic birds, and football-playing elephants. Yes, the top-of-the-bill attraction, 'the greatest novelty in the world', was an elephants versus clowns football match. And, when the circus rolled into Leicester in March 1899, there was an added attraction – an elephant versus man penalty shoot-out. 'For a MASSIVE GOBLET, which will be on view at Mr Russell's Music Warehouse,' the playbill announced, 'Mr W KEECH, Loughborough Football Club, has arranged to compete against SANGER'S CENTRE-FORWARD ELEPHANT, which can kick the most goals out of five tries. Mr W KEECH and the ELEPHANT to keep goal in turn.' Who among the good folk of Leicester would not pay sixpence to watch that? William Keech was a bona fide professional footballer – a former Liverpool half-back, who had recently left Leicester Fosse for Loughborough. The elephant, named Palm, was a natural goalkeeper – being that it was big enough to fill the goalmouth – and a pretty good goalscorer, too. It was said that Palm was entirely invincible, and in Leicester three professional footballers were duly sent away flushed with embarrassment after being beaten by the mighty beast. Then up stepped Keech. According to legend, Keech used a well-practised penalty technique to somehow send the virtually immoveable elephant the wrong way. Indeed, after two kicks Keech held a 2-0 lead. However, Palm was no mug. Having figured out Keech's game, the elephant proceeded to send the footballer the wrong way. After four kicks, the score was 2-2. Keech scored his final penalty, and then, heroically, saved the elephant's last kick. Keech won 3-2, and was presented with the 'MASSIVE GOB-LET'. But an elephant never forgets. And, so the story goes, Palm was never beaten ever again.

CHARLES CLEGG

Known as the 'Napoleon of football', John Charles Clegg was born in Sheffield in 1850. Alongside younger brother William, Clegg was influential in developing the Sheffield game. He acted as president and chairman of Sheffield Wednesday, Sheffield United and the Sheffield FA (and in later life also became mayor of Sheffield). A fine player, he made his name at Sheffield FC, and was one of only two northerners representing England in the first international match in 1872. Clegg was virtually ignored by his Southern teammates, who he described as 'awful snobs'. A successful solicitor, Clegg became one of the leading referees of the Victorian era, developing a no-nonsense reputation. Having been prominent committee member, and one who strongly opposed professionalism, Clegg was appointed chairman of the FA in 1890, a position he held until his death in 1937. He was regarded as a tough leader during difficult times for football. 'The game owes more to Mr Clegg than any man can compute,' wrote Jimmy Catton. 'Such as he are the salt of the game.'

FA LEADERS

President:

Arthur Pember	1863–67
Ebenezer Cobb Morley	1867–74
Francis Marindin	1874–90
Arthur Kinnaird	1890–1923

Secretary:

Ebenezer Cobb Morley	1863–66
RW Willis	1866–68
RG Graham	1868–70
CW Alcock	1870–95
Frederick Wall	1895–1934

Chairman:

Charles Clegg	1890–1937

CALCIO

Football had been played in Italy since Roman times, and was codified in Florence in the 16th century as a complicated kicking game called *Calcio Fiorentino*. Association football was brought to Italy by Turin textile merchant Edoardo Bosio, who became a fan of the game while working in England. In 1887, Bosio formed the Torino Football and Cricket Club, recruiting employees from his textile firm. Another club, Nobili Torino, was formed shortly afterwards by local noblemen, including the famous Duke of Abruzzi. The two clubs merged in 1891 to form Internazionale Torino. Turin became an early centre of Italian football, with other local clubs such as FBC Torinese and Ginnastica Torino emerging. Elsewhere, the Genoa Cricket and Athletics Club was formed in 1893. However, it wasn't until 1897 that British doctor James Richardson Spensley, a medic for British coal shipping firms, set up a football section. Genoa played its first game in 1898 against a combined Internazionale Torino / FBC Torinese side, and lost 1-0. Later that year, the Federazione Italiana Football (FIF) was formed. Spensley was keenly involved, and he organised the first Italian Football Championship, also in 1898. Genoa and the three Turin clubs participated in the four-team knockout tournament, with Spensley's Genoa beating Bosio's Internazionale Torino 2-1 after extra time in the final. Genoa won the first three Italian championships, and survives today as Italy's oldest football club. Italy's most successful clubs, Juventus and AC Milan, were founded in 1897 and 1899 respectively. Juventus was formed in the football hotbed of Turin as Sport Club Juventus by schoolboys from the Massimo D'Azeglio Lyceum. 'Juventus' is the Latin word for youth. The club originally wore pink shirts, only switching to black and white stripes in 1906. AC Milan was formed as Milan Football and Cricket Club in 1899 by Alfred Edwards and Herbert Kiplin, two expatriates from Nottingham. Kilpin was a lace merchant who had previously worked for Edoardo Bosio and played for Internazionale Torino in Turin.

SEEDS OF CHANGE

'The connection between football and canary seeds is not very obvious,' began an intriguing 'Strange But True!' column in the *Children's Friend*, 'but in a recent report of the London Agricultural Seed Market the steady decrease in the sale of canary seeds is attributed to the growing popularity of football in the north of England. In that part of the country large numbers of people who used formerly to keep cage birds, now give all their spare time and interest to football.'

REFEREE EGGED

Pity poor William Hay, referee of a match involving Moffat FC in Dumfries in 1897, who was 'mobbed and shamefully treated' at the final whistle. In a subsequent court session it was revealed that he had been threatened, seized, and pelted with eggs. Five defendants were fined a pound each for throwing eggs, while another was fined two pounds for attempting to pull the ref's nose.

QUEEN IS DEAD

Following the death of Queen Victoria on 22 January 1901, the FA issued a circular postponing all FA Cup ties. The decision was unpopular with many clubs, 'because the postponement interfered with their arrangements and seemed to point to financial loss'. 'If any proof had been wanted of the sordid interests of the promoters of professional football,' said the *Penny Illustrated*, 'it could not have come in more unquestionable shape than the objection raised to the course pursued by the officers of the FA.' Professional clubs, the paper said, 'regard the "gate" as the be-all and end-all of football'. The Football League, meanwhile, decided not to postpone any matches, except for on the day of the Queen's funeral.

OLYMPIC GOLD

Football was included as an exhibition sport at the second modern Olympic Games in Paris in September 1900. Great Britain was represented by a now-defunct club side, and no medals were ever awarded. Nevertheless, Britain has been retrospectively recorded as the first official Olympic football champion. It was originally intended that five nations would participate in the football event, which was part of Paris's grand Exposition Universelle. However, Germany and Switzerland decided not to send teams, leaving only France, Belgium and Great Britain. The hosts were represented by a national XI selected by governing body the Union des Sociétés Françaises de Sports Athlétiques (USFSA). Belgium was represented by players from several University teams. The side selected to represent Great Britain was Upton Park, a club that had been around since 1866, but had never been particularly successful. The keenly amateur Upton Park had no connection to West Ham United (then Thames Ironworks) or to West Ham's Boleyn Ground (also known as Upton Park). The obscure and forgotten nature of the team's players is indicated by the fact that the name of its captain is variously recorded as 'A Haslam', 'HA Harlan' and 'HN Haslow'. More clearly identified were JH Jones in goal, and international cricket star Percy Buckenham at right-back. Outside-right Arthur Turner was brought in for the Games from Crouch End Vampires. Upton Park only actually played one match in Paris, comfortably beating the USFSA XI. The East London team won 4-0 at the Vélodromme de Vincennes in Paris, with two goals from J Nicholas and a goal each from James Zeally and Arthur Turner. The match was largely ignored by British newspapers. Three days later, the USFSA XI defeated the Belgian side 6-1. That meant the British and French teams had won one game each, and everyone went home with no thought of triumphs or medals. It was only later decided that Great Britain had 'won', whether on win percentage or goal difference. Upton Park were Olympic champions.

BILLY MEREDITH

Billy Meredith's long football career began in 1890 in Chirk in North Wales, where he worked as a pit pony driver while playing for Chirk AAA FC. The 'Welsh Wizard' joined Manchester City in 1894, scoring 12 goals in his first season, before being appointed club captain in his second – aged just 21. Meredith led City into the first division, scoring 29 league goals in 1898-99, and established himself as a Welsh international. A 'crafty dribbler', his form and longevity were attributed to dedicated training, and the fact that he never touched cigarettes or alcohol. Meredith went on to become one of the most important footballers of the 20th century. After being involved in an infamous bribery scandal, he was transferred from Manchester City to Manchester United. He won two league titles and the FA Cup with United, before finishing his career back at City. Meredith was also central to the formation of the Association Football Player's Association. He continued to play football until he was almost 50 years old.

VICTORIAN FOOTBALL TIMELINE

1842: CW Alcock born.

1847: Arthur Kinnaird born.

1846: Football banned in Derby.

1848: Cambridge Rules created.

1857: Sheffield FC (oldest amateur club) formed.

1858: Sheffield Rules created.

1859: Wanderers formed.

1862: Notts County (oldest professional club) formed.

1863: Football Association formed.
Laws of the Game published.

1867: Queen's Park (oldest Scottish club) formed.
Youdan Cup (first football tournament) played.

1870: First 'Alcock International' played.

1871: FA Cup initiated.

1872: First FA Cup final, Wanderers 1-0 Royal Engineers.

1872: First international match, Scotland 0-0 England.

1873: Scottish Football Association formed.

1876: Cambrian Football Association (Football Association of Wales) formed.

1880: Irish Football Association formed.

1884: British Home Championship begins.

1885: Professionalism legalised.

1886: International Football Association Board formed.

1888: Football League founded.
Solid crossbars replace tapes.

1889: Northern League founded.
Football Alliance founded.

1890: Scottish Football League formed.

1891: Penalty kick and goal nets introduced.
Referee and linesman roles defined.

1892: Football League incorporates Football Alliance as second division.

1895: Southern League founded.

1900: Great Britain wins Olympic football exhibition.

FURTHER READING

Association Football and How to Play It, John Cameron
    (Health and Strength, 1908)
Association Football and the Men Who Made It, Alfred Gibson
    and William Pickford (Caxton, 1906)
The Association Game: A History of British Football,
    Dr Matthew Taylor (Pearson, 2007)
Beastly Fury: The Strange Birth of British Football,
    Richard Sanders (Bantam, 2009)
Denied FC, Dave Twydell (Yore Publications, 2001)
First Elevens: The Birth of International Football,
    Andy Mitchell (Andy Mitchell Media, 2012)
Football: The First Hundred Years, Adrian Harvey
    (Routledge, 2005)
The Football Association 1863-1883: A Source Book,
    Tony Brown (Soccerdata, 2011)
Football Through the Turnstiles Again, Brian Tabner (Yore, 2002)
Goal-Post: Victorian Football, ed. Paul Brown (Superelastic, 2012)
Sheffield FC: Celebrating 150 Years, Steve Hutton, Graham Curry
    and Peter Goodman (At Heart Ltd, 2005)
The Story of Association Football (Wickets and Goals),
    Tityrus (JAH Catton) (Chapman and Hall, 1926)
The Wanderers: Five Times FA Cup Winners, Rob Cavallini
    (Dog n Duck, 2005)
See also Victorian Football Books, page 64

Websites:
Archives of the IFAB, www.ssbra.org/html/laws/ifab.html
Association Football Before the D,
    www.gottfriedfuchs.blogspot.co.uk
Historical Football Kits, www.historicalkits.co.uk
The Rec.Sport.Soccer Statistics Foundation, www.rsssf.com
Soccerdata History, www.soccer.mistral.co.uk/hist1.htm
Soccer History, www.soccerhistory.org.uk
Spartacus Educational Football Encyclopaedia,
    www.spartacus.schoolnet.co.uk/ENCfootball.htm
Soccerbase, www.soccerbase.com
Victorian Football, www.victorianfootball.co.uk
Wisconsin Soccer Central, www.wisconsinsoccercentral.com

INDEX

Printed in Great Britain
by Amazon.co.uk, Ltd.,
Marston Gate.